THE
CHOCOLATE
COMPANION
A CONNOISSEUR'S GUIDE

by Chantal Coady

Foreword by Robert Linxe

SECOND EDITION

D0188213

THE
CHOCOLATE
COMPANION

A CONNOISSEUR'S GUIDE

by Chantal Coady

Updated by Martin Christy
Foreword by Robert Linxe

SECOND EDITION

RUNNING PRESS
PHILADELPHIA • LONDON

DEDICATION

To James, my husband, Fergus and Millie, our beloved children, and all the wonderful
chocolate makers around the world who have inspired me
and from whom I have learnt so much.

A QUINTET BOOK

Copyright © 2006 Quintet Publishing Limited.
First published in the United States of America in 2006 by
Running Press Book Publishers.

9 8 7 6 5 4 3 2 1
Digit on the right indicates the number of this printing
Library of Congress Cataloging-in-Publication Number 2006920941

ISBN-13: 978-0-7624-2897-7
ISBN-10: 0-7624-2897-X

This book was designed and produced by
Quintet Publishing Limited
6 Blundell Street
London N7 9BH

Project Editor Second Edition: **Victoria Wiggins**
Project Editor First Edition: **Laura Sandelson**
Designer: **Rod Teasdale**
Photographers: **Phil Wilkins, Paul Forrester**
Creative Director: **Richard Dewing**
Managing Editor: **Jane Laing**
Publisher: **Judith More**

This book may be ordered by mail from the publisher.
But try your bookstore first!

Running Press Book Publishers
125 South Twenty-second Street
Philadelphia, Pennsylvania 19103-4399
Visit us on the web!
www.runningpresscooks.com
www.runningpress.com

Manufactured in Singapore by Pica Digital Pte. Ltd.
Printed in China by SNP Leefung Printers Ltd.

AUTHOR ACKNOWLEDGMENTS
To Robert Linxe, for his vision and inspiration;
to Martin Christy for all his hard work, support and enthusiasm to update this edition;
and to Chloe Doutre Roussel, and our other fellow academicians at the AoC.

CONTENTS

FOREWORD

A large part of my life has been dedicated to chocolate, and I am very flattered that
Chantal Coady should have asked me to write the foreword to her book.
She is a friend who, I am certain, has produced a book that will
encompass every reader's expectations of chocolate—a foodstuff
that has become an obsession throughout the world.

Chocolate is a marvelous product, embued with so many virtues:
first its energetic value, which can be attributed to the magnesium, potassium,
and vitamin A, as well as theobromine, a healthy antidepressant that is
uplifting and can be a wonderful way of dispelling gloom.

Then there is the attraction for the gourmet, but this depends on the chocolate
being of the very finest quality. Quality is determined by the provenance
of the cocoa beans, the manufacture of the couverture, and finally
on the creation of fine chocolate bonbons.

To achieve a balance that will satisfy the tastebuds, as much rigorous
discipline and vigilance are necessary with chocolate as they
are with any field of virtuosity. I believe that without love
or passion nothing great or beautiful can be achieved.

To create a great product is not an easy thing:
I have sacrificed much because I refuse to
compromise quality;
one should never accept mediocrity.

I wish Chantal Coady all the success she deserves
for this magnificent book that has
involved so much hard work.

With my warmest congratulations and sincere good wishes.

Robert Linxe
Paris
March 1995

THE
STORY OF
CHOCOLATE

Part One

THE HISTORY OF CHOCOLATE

Hernando Cortés and his Spanish army are greeted by the Aztec Emperor, Montezuma.

Few people biting into a piece of chocolate today would stop to consider that this epicurean delight has Aztec connections and was introduced into sixteenth-century Europe through carnage, bloodshed, and ruthless exploitation.

In the name of the Spanish Crown in 1519, an adventurous conquistador by the name of Hernando Cortés landed on the coast of Veracruz with only a few hundred men, horses, and cannon. On reaching the Aztec capital, Tenochtitlán (now Mexico City), they were astounded by the civilization they found there. But only two years later, through Spanish ruthlessness, superior military technology, some heroism, and a lot of luck, the indigenous population was decimated, its wealth plundered, and the centuries-old empire in tatters. Whatever the final cataclysm predicted in Aztec mythology, the Spaniards had meted out a conclusive end to the Aztec Emperor Montezuma's bloodthirsty regime.

Cortés left the smoldering ruins of Tenochtitlán with a vast knowledge of the Aztec civilization that he had destroyed, and one aspect that particularly intrigued him was the Aztecs' consumption of a strange brew known as *xocolatl*. Although Columbus had earlier introduced cocoa beans and the Aztec version of the drink to his patrons, King Ferdinand and Queen Isabella, the bitter, scummy, and peppery drink had been intensely disliked, and the court's attention had been rapidly absorbed by another novelty on the Santa María's inventory: a Native American. Some 20 years later, Cortés finally caught the imagination of Holy Roman Emperor Charles V and his courtiers with his own, modified version of *xocolatl*. He added sugar and vanilla to the brew, and recounted stirring tales of Montezuma tossing discarded golden goblets into the lake after imbibing the sacred drink. His success in introducing molten chocolate as a drink established a new era in the history of chocolate consumption.

The golden goblets of *xocolatl* that Cortés had tasted at the end of the sumptuous banquets given in his honor by Montezuma were very different from the drinking chocolate we are familiar with today. *Xocolatl* literally means "bitter water," and if you ever have the opportunity to taste a cocoa nib (the inside of the bean), you will understand how appropriate the name is. The Aztecs mixed chiles and other native spices and flowers with the dried, roasted, and ground cocoa nibs. Cornmeal was then added as a basic emulsifier to absorb the greasy cocoa butter.

On ceremonial occasions, Montezuma would demand large quantities of *xocolatl*, often a thousand jugfuls in a single night. Jugs would be mixed from a prepared block of the processed nibs—a crude sort of chocolate tablet. It is clear from Spanish records that Montezuma drank *xocolatl* as a tonic aphrodisiac. This precious concoction was not only strictly reserved for men; it was also only available to the elite—it was "liquid gold." Cocoa beans became a common form of currency, and four nibs could buy a rabbit, 10 the company of a "lady of the night," and 100 a slave. Given how much the nibs were worth, it is not surprising that hollowed-out cocoa-bean shells filled with earth were the currency among pre-Columbian fraudsters. Interestingly, this practice has endured thoughout the history of cocoa and chocolate, and persists to this day in more subtle forms. Witness today's industrially produced "chocolate" and you will see that not much has changed...

At first, cocoa was grown only by the Maya people, who had been subjects of the Aztecs from about AD 1200. Botanists believe that the first cocoa trees grew wild in the shade of the tropical rainforests of the Amazon and Orinoco basins approximately 4,000 years ago, and that they were first cultivated by the Maya when they migrated west to the warm, humid, low-lying Yucatán peninsula in the seventh century AD. When the Aztecs conquered large parts of Mexico 700 years later, they imposed a feudal system on their subjugated tribes— whereby all taxes were paid in cocoa beans.

Temple of the Sun in the Aztec capital, Tenochtitlán.

COMMERCIAL CULTIVATION

Cortés and his men had gone to Mexico in search of *el dorado* (literally, "the gilded"), but although there were large quantities of gold in the Aztec treasury, they did not find the vast wealth they had dreamed of. Having seen cocoa beans being used as a medium of exchange, and noting the esteem in which the Aztecs held the drink for its restorative and aphrodisiac properties, Cortés put his mind to the possibilities of commercially exploiting this "liquid gold." He soon established cocoa plantations across a wide area—from Mexico to Trinidad and Haiti. Cortés is also reputed to have initiated cultivation on an island off the coast of West Africa during one of his return voyages to Spain, and it was from there that cultivation spread to the Gold Coast in 1879. Latin America and West Africa continue to be the principal areas of cocoa cultivation.

When the Spanish first colonized the New World, a huge percentage of the indigenous population fell victim to the ravages of Western diseases. As a result, the colonists—having already overexploited the Native Americans as slave labor—were faced with a diminishing workforce, and the Spanish had to explore other means of "recruitment." In time, African slaves were to become as important to cocoa cultivation as they were to the burgeoning sugar industry in other parts of the Americas; however, during the seventeenth and eighteenth centuries, Brazil and Venezuela continued to suffer from a shortage of labor.

Other important sources of production were Peru and the rest of the Caribbean basin, but all cocoa exported to Spain and Mexico was liable to taxation. The Spanish Crown proved to be no less calculating than the Aztecs had been.

Cocoa pods growing at the Belmont Estate plantation in Grenada.

EUROPEAN TASTES

For the first hundred years after its discovery by Europeans, cocoa remained more or less the preserve of the Spanish court. It was very expensive and could only have been afforded by those in aristocratic circles, whether in the New World viceroyalties or in Spain itself. This monopoly was gradually broken during the first half of the seventeenth century. Because of the Spanish Hapsburg connection (the Hapsburg Charles I of Spain had also been Holy Roman Emperor Charles V), news of the drink spread to Germany, Austria, and Flanders, and subsequently to France. An Italian, Antonio Carletti, who had traveled to the Spanish-American possessions, introduced cocoa to Italy in 1606. Reactions were mixed. In countries where it was well established, it was regarded as a wholesome drink; though an early English reference by the herbalist John Parkinson labels it "a wash fitter for hogs." Opinions would soon change, but few people today on tasting the 1640 mixture of cocoa beans, sugar, cinnamon, red pepper, cloves, logwood (a type of fennel), and aniseed would disagree with this early critique. There are even reports of pirates who jettisoned cargoes of cocoa beans into Caribbean waters believing them to be sacks of sheep dung!

In 1660, a Franco-Spanish alliance was established when Anne of Austria (Austria being, at this time, a Spanish possession), married Louis XIII of France. The alliance was further strengthened by the marriage of María Theresa to Louis XIV, the Sun King. Her maid—brought specially from Spain to prepare chocolate in the Queen's apartments—was nicknamed "la molina" for the "molinillo" stick that had been used since the days of the Aztecs to beat the chocolate into a froth. Chocolate was restricted to the inner sanctum of courtiers, who were invited to partake of a bowl of chocolate during the ritual early morning "levées": a sort of glorified breakfast in bed.

Socializing over cocoa in the early 1800s.

Another shift in dynastic politics occurred in 1711, when the Holy Roman Emperor Charles VI transferred his court from Madrid to Vienna. With the court came the Spanish penchant for chocolate, and Vienna was to become famous for its rich cups of chocolate served with glasses of chilled water and later, of course, for the Hotel Sacher's chocolate cake, the Sachertorte.

Chocolate appears to have reached London in about 1650, spreading quite rapidly during the reign of the merry monarch, Charles II, while acquiring a reputation as a nourishing drink. Pepys describes it in his diary notes for April 24, 1661 as a hangover cure on the morning after the coronation of the King. One of the King's physicians, Henry Stubbe, extolled the benefits of chocolate. He indicates that even then there were two varieties: ordinary and royal. Royal chocolate contained a high percentage of cocoa and relatively little sugar.

By the 1660s, with the omission of most of the spices, chocolate as drunk by the Spanish and English courts bore some resemblance to our current conception of it, albeit a rather greasy one. In Spain, one ounce of chocolate, two of sugar, and eight fluid ounces of water were mixed, heated, and whipped to a froth. Indeed, the modern version of the Spanish *chocolate a la piedra* (a stone-ground drinking chocolate in tablet form) contains maize or rice flour, as favored by the Aztecs. In France, milk often replaced half of the water, while English chocolate houses used either milk or egg.

During the eighteenth century, Europe saw a rapid increase in chocolate consumption. In England, at the start of the century, only wealthy people could afford to drink it, since it was heavily taxed with stiff fines or prison sentences for anyone trying to evade customs officers. This inevitably led, as it had in Aztec times, to adulteration: starch, cocoa shells, and even brick dust might find their way into the cocoa. It is sad that in some countries, even today, for commercial reasons, you can find bars labeled as "chocolate" when they contain as little as 15 percent cocoa solids. There are few other products where this sort of deception is possible, and I hope that in due course consumer awareness will force a reduction of the large amounts of sugar and other non-cocoa products that are used in some "chocolate" manufacture.

Despite high levels of taxation, the charms of chocolate won through. By 1852, duty on colonial cocoa in England had decreased from two shillings (24 pennies) to one penny per

Belgian Suchard poster, circa 1905.

pound, partly as a result of Quaker industrialist claims of cocoa's merits, and partly due to the large volume being imported. In 1850, 1,400 tons of cocoa were brought into Britain, and by the turn of the century this had multiplied almost ninefold. Not only were cocoa and drinking chocolate now much more affordable, but they had become big business. Many of the early cocoa entrepreneurs are now household names: Hershey, Cadbury, Fry, and Rowntree to name but a few. They all owe a debt to Swiss pioneer inventors such as Cailler, Suchard, Peter, Nestlé, Lindt, and Tobler.

FOUNDING FATHERS OF THE SWISS CHOCOLATE INDUSTRY

| François-Louis Cailler | Daniel Peter | Henri Nestlé | Rodolphe Lindt |

THE AMERICAN MARKET

Baker's original cocoa packaging was inspired by the 1740s painting, "The chocolate girl," by the Swiss painter Jean-Etienne Liotard.

B ig business has always been a feature of the American chocolate industry. The first news of chocolate in North America seems to have arrived in the middle of the eighteenth century. In 1765, the first factory was opened in Massachusetts by Dr James Baker and John Hannon. Baker's grandson, Walter, established the Walter Baker Company in 1780, and "Baker's" remains synonymous with quality chocolate in the United States. On the West Coast, however, Ghirardelli is the byword. From humble beginnings supplying groceries to the gold rush hordes, Domenico Ghirardelli later specialized in chocolate. By 1885, he was importing the huge amount of 200 tons of cocoa beans annually for his California Chocolate Manufactory. The buildings of the original factory—Ghirardelli Square in San Francisco—remain a famous landmark for tourists.

For the United States as a whole, however, it is Milton Hershey's chocolate that is probably best known. In fact, at the outset of his career, Hershey

was not directly involved in chocolate, but was instead considered the caramel king of the East Coast. Influenced perhaps by the chocolate stands at the World's Columbus Exposition of 1892 (an exhibition to celebrate the 400th centenary of Columbus' landing in the New World), he decided that he would make chocolate the snack food of the future. He sold his caramel factory for one million dollars and built a village and chocolate bar factory at Hersheyville—modeled on Cadbury's Bournville in Birmingham, England. Ever the visionary entrepreneur, Hershey invented a milk chocolate bar with almonds, and was the first manufacturer to experiment with the use of solid vegetable fats which raised the melting point of a chocolate bar so that it could still be sold in the tropical heat of an American summer, or even shipped to the troops as daily rations during World War II. Hydrogenated fats are still in widespread use among industrial chocolate makers but, thanks to pressure groups, things are now changing for the better.

Ghirardelli's bittersweet chocolate and cocoa is still available in American stores.

QUAKER INDUSTRIALISTS

The Cadbury family was one of the four great Quaker families (along with the Frys, Terrys, and Rowntrees) who became involved with cocoa, primarily because they saw it as a flourishing and healthy alternative to the menace of Dutch gin. These families played a large part in extending the consumption of cocoa and chocolate beyond the rich and aristocratic, making it a food of the people. The drink was promoted as a wholesome "flesh-forming" substance, and certainly with its history as a restorative and tonic, this was a valid enough claim—even if it rings a little odd to our ears today. Another extraordinary element in what these Quaker industrialists were offering was the provision of model working environments and housing for their workers, as part of their campaign for more justice and humanity in society. As nonconformists to the established church, the Quakers had been barred from the great universities of the day, and from medicine and law. Industry provided an outlet for their enormous energy, and subsequently their profits were used to air the Quaker views on labor reform on a wider scale. It was ironic that much of this profit was derived from slave-grown cocoa in West Africa, and when this was pointed out by a journalist in 1908, a celebrated libel trial began. The Cadburys won derisive damages of a farthing, but the affair did eventually lead to some improvement in working conditions on the plantations.

Bournville Green, Birmingham, England. The model village was built for Cadbury's workers in 1878.

THE MAGIC OF CHOCOLATE

Charlie is amazed to find a golden ticket inside his Willy Wonka bar of Fudge Mallow Delight.

Throughout the closing years of the nineteenth century and up to the present day, chocolate has grown to be an integral part of the daily culture of all levels of society in the Western world. The very word conjures up warm, comforting images, never more so than in wartime. From the Boer War of the 1890s onward through the two World Wars, the morale of both troops and population was maintained by the chocolate ration. Who has not read Roald Dahl's *Charlie and the Chocolate Factory* without in some way empathizing with the starving Charlie Bucket as he bites into his bar of Fudge Mallow Delight, and finally goes on his voyage of discovery and triumph in the heart of Willy Wonka's magical world of chocolate?

Soldiers take respite with a bar of chocolate.

THE MAKING OF CHOCOLATE

THE COCOA TREE

Linnaeus classified the cocoa tree *Theobroma cacao*: an indication of the spell that chocolate was able to cast over even a hardened scientist. The word *Theobroma* means "food of the gods," so it is no dry appellation. Perhaps Linnaeus had in mind the role of cocoa in Aztec ritual, its impressive list of mineral ingredients, or even its reputed aphrodisiac qualities. Had he foreseen the modern generation bingeing on the sugar-laden "chocolate" candy bar, who knows what label he would have given it?

The cocoa tree, a native species of the Amazon rainforests, grows in the tropics in a belt approximately 20 degrees north and south of the equator. To thrive, it needs sunshine and warmth, and young trees must be sheltered from the full heat of the sun and, above all, from the wind. Cultivation in the Caribbean is made very difficult by the hurricanes that regularly strike the area. Just one day of wind can leave a cocoa plantation fruitless for years. On modern plantations, the rows of cocoa trees are often mixed with coconut palms and banana trees that provide shade. This also has the effect of limiting the height of the trees to no more than about 20 feet, making the harvest easier.

In favorable conditions, both fruit and flowers may be carried throughout the year. Only a small percentage of the tens of thousands of flowers give rise to fruit: the pods that contain the seeds, we call cocoa beans. The pods are the shape of a miniature football and can grow up to 12 inches long and 5 inches across, turning a deep red or yellow color when ripe. For commercial reasons, there are two main annual harvests. The first starts toward the end of the rainy season and continues through to the beginning of the dry season, and a smaller second harvest takes place at the start of the following rainy season. The pods have to be cut carefully from the tree with machetes, ensuring that no damage is done to the tree itself—disease can easily be introduced into small cuts in the bark. This is labor-intensive work and generally very poorly rewarded.

FRUITS OF THE HARVEST

The harvested pods are sliced open, revealing rows of fleshy white fruit. The fruit is placed in vats and the high sugar content of the flesh precipitates fermentation. The fleshy pulp surrounding the seeds turns into acetic acid that evaporates, leaving behind the fermented light brown, "green" cocoa beans, which are about the size of a fat almond and look a bit like litchi nuts. This is the process during which characteristic chocolate "notes" are developed; a process similar to that of the fermentation of grapes in wine making.

The cocoa pod contains fleshy white fruit.

The beans are spread out in big trays to dry.

After preparing the beans for transportation, the second stage is drying, which is best done naturally in the open air—sometimes with rolling covers to protect from sudden rain. In areas where rainfall is unpredictable, the beans are often dried in ovens, but there is always some danger of contamination from wood smoke or the fumes of other fuel: cocoa beans easily pick up foreign flavors. Valrhona—the specialist producer in France's Rhône Valley—refuses to buy beans that have been oven dried, because their smoky taste can be so pervasive that even a tiny number of smoky beans can ruin a whole batch of chocolate. The dried beans, now weighing a quarter of the harvest weight, are packed into 110-pound sacks ready for shipment.

It is worth remembering that today cocoa, like coffee, is an internationally traded commodity. The vast bulk of the world's production is handled by a few multinational companies, and for this reason only a handful of specialist producers can keep complete control of the quality of the beans they use by sourcing the best beans on the best plantations. The quality and price of their finished products reflect this commercial situation and, invariably, you will get what you pay for.

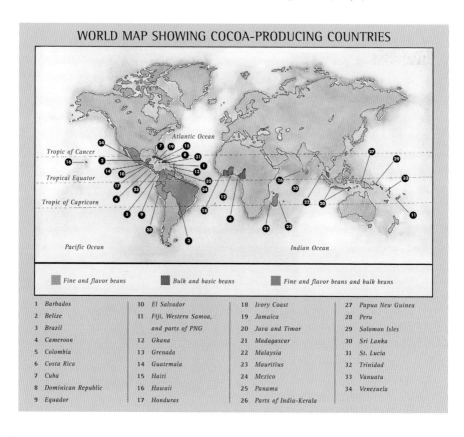

WORLD MAP SHOWING COCOA-PRODUCING COUNTRIES

Atlantic Ocean

Tropic of Cancer

Tropical Equator

Tropic of Capricorn

Pacific Ocean

Indian Ocean

Fine and flavor beans   Bulk and basic beans   Fine and flavor beans and bulk beans

1	Barbados	10	El Salvador	18	Ivory Coast	27	Papua New Guinea
2	Belize	11	Fiji, Western Samoa,	19	Jamaica	28	Peru
3	Brazil		and parts of PNG	20	Java and Timor	29	Solomon Isles
4	Cameroon	12	Ghana	21	Madagascar	30	Sri Lanka
5	Colombia	13	Grenada	22	Malaysia	31	St. Lucia
6	Costa Rica	14	Guatemala	23	Mauritius	32	Trinidad
7	Cuba	15	Haiti	24	Mexico	33	Vanuatu
8	Dominican Republic	16	Hawaii	25	Panama	34	Venezuela
9	Equador	17	Honduras	26	Parts of India-Kerala		

THE CHOCOLATE FACTORY

On arriving at the chocolate factory, the beans are carefully checked and sorted. They are sometimes dried again to eliminate the residual 10 percent or so moisture and will then, like coffee, be carefully roasted to develop their flavor. Again as with coffee, the poorer quality beans will be roasted at higher temperatures to disguise their inadequacies. Each batch of beans that is to be used in a particular blend of chocolate is roasted separately. Even the mass producers of cheap chocolate use a blend of beans—sometimes called a "cuvée"—to create their particular taste; and the process is similar to blending two or more grape varieties to make a wine, or blending malts to make a whiskey. Unlike wine or whiskey, however, it was until very recently almost unheard of to use a single bean to make chocolate. Another term that has been borrowed from the wine industry is "cru," which literally means growth, and as with champagne, refers to a particular, usually good-quality plantation. "Grand Cru," a term first coined by Valrhona, is an extension of this idea—meaning a plantation producing the very finest cocoa beans. Certainly Valrhona's Grand Cru chocolates are made with extraordinary care and attention to detail, and their blending panel of 12 chocolate experts meets every day to guarantee the consistency and quality of their products.

After being checked and then roasted, the beans are winnowed to remove their outer skins, leaving behind the nib, or kernel. The making of chocolate or cocoa can now begin in earnest. The nibs are ground by passing them through a series of rollers. At this point, the beans will be subjected to one of two separate processes. A large manufacturer of quality chocolate will need extra cocoa butter to add in the final stages of chocolate production, and is also likely to sell cocoa powder for cooking and drinking. Therefore, in one process, the ground nibs are hydraulically pressed and the cocoa butter melts, leaving behind a cocoa powder "cake," which

The beans are checked and sorted on arrival.

may be further pressed and refined, although most cocoa powder contains some fat.

In the other process, the nibs are ground into a fine paste that then goes into a mixer with sugar, extra cocoa butter, real vanilla or artificial ethyl vanillin, soy lecithin as an emulsifier, and milk products if appropriate. The mixer pulverizes and kneads together the individual particles of chocolate that are, at this stage, between 50 and 70 microns in size (a micron is one thousandth of a millimeter), and still noticeably gritty on the palate. To make it taste completely smooth and silky, the mixture then has to be conched—a process invented by the Swiss, Rodolphe Lindt, in 1880. The name is derived from the shape of his prototype, a large shell-shaped vessel, inside which granite rollers further grind the chocolate to a smooth, velvety texture—reducing the particle size to 18 to 20 microns, which is indiscernible to the palate. Conching also helps to take away any remaining bitterness by aerating the chocolate. It takes only 12 hours if commercial considerations are the principal motivating force, although it may take 3 to 4 days if you are a perfectionist.

A melangeur refines the beans before conching.

The final step is to temper the chocolate. This involves melting it completely at about 122°F (50°C) to break down the crystalline structure of the cocoa butter, then cooling it to about 86°F (30°C) to reintroduce the structure, and finally raising the temperature slightly so that the crystals join up again in perfect chains. Exact temperatures depend on the type of chocolate, but the effect is to leave the finished chocolate with a well-rounded flavor, and means that it is easy to mold, has a good sheen, and will keep well.

This, then, is the basic traditional process. There are, of course, many variations on it, as well as multiple ways of cutting corners and economizing. It is most unusual for an artisan producer—as with Bernachon of Lyon—to do all the drying, roasting, winnowing, and conching on the premises. Quality is never compromised.

CHOCOLATE INGREDIENTS

Plain chocolate is made up of two key raw materials: cocoa beans and sugar. Partly through the efforts of the producers of fine chocolate, it is in vogue to talk about the cocoa content of a chocolate bar as if it were the only factor that influences the quality of the finished product. It is perfectly possible, however, to produce low-quality chocolate with a high cocoa content; in my opinion, most chocolate with a cocoa content of more than 85 percent is extremely unpalatable, and the optimum range is between 55 and 75 percent. What is vitally important is the quality of the beans, and perhaps the greatest skill is in deciding how much sugar to mix with a particular blend of fine beans. Economic considerations are also likely to affect decision making, because sugar is five times cheaper than cocoa beans and more than 10 times cheaper than cocoa butter.

As with coffee, there are two main varieties of bean. The thin-skinned *criollo* (the Spanish for "domestic") is the equivalent of the arabica bean, and it is this rarer, less hardy, and lower flavor-yielding bean that represents, at the most, 10 percent of the world's production. It is grown in Venezuela, the Caribbean, the Indian Ocean, Indonesia, and Madagascar. These small trees bear long, medium-sized, deeply grooved pods that taper to a fine point.

The thicker skinned *forastero* ("foreign") is akin to the robusta coffee bean and is widely cultivated in Africa and Brazil. Similarly robust and lacking in flavor, it requires vigorous roasting to disguise its inadequacies. It is this high roasting that gives a burnt taste and aroma to much dark chocolate. The best producers do use some forastero beans in their blends, because they give body and breadth to the chocolate, but it is the criollo bean that gives acidity, balance, and complexity to the finest chocolate.

It is generally true that when there is less than 50 percent cocoa solids in dark chocolate, it is unlikely to be of the best quality: it will either be too sweet, or fats and other cocoa

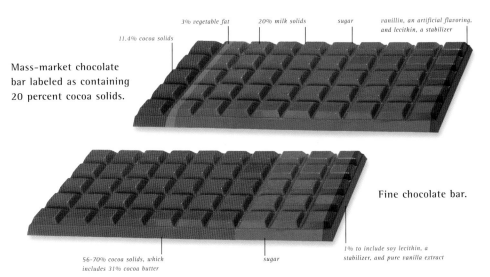

3% vegetable fat   20% milk solids   sugar   vanillin, an artificial flavoring, and lecithin, a stabilizer

11.4% cocoa solids

Mass-market chocolate bar labeled as containing 20 percent cocoa solids.

Fine chocolate bar.

56-70% cocoa solids, which includes 31% cocoa butter

sugar

1% to include soy lecithin, a stabilizer, and pure vanilla extract

butter "enhancers" (as they are euphemistically known) will replace a proportion of the cocoa butter content. Why substitute the cocoa butter? Various reasons for substituting the cocoa butter are given by the mass producers, such as improvement in shelf-life or increasing the melting point. One reason is undoubtedly financial, for cocoa butter is valued by the cosmetics industry as a unique fat; it melts at just below blood temperature, which makes it a perfect base for lipstick and other creams. It is this aspect of cocoa butter that gives chocolate its sensual feel in the mouth, and it is something that no other ingredient can adequately replace. If you try a cheap commercial bar, watch out for the cloying, greasy residue on the roof of your mouth—it is probably caused by the palm or nut fats, or other cocoa butter substitutes. The cocoa butter's crystalline structure also gives fine chocolate its distinctive snap on breaking, its luster, and its fine sheen. Although a saturated fat, cocoa butter contains a high proportion of unsaturated fatty acids and has a neutral effect on blood cholesterol levels.

Dark chocolate with less than 50 percent cocoa solids content is inevitably going to be too sweet. Michel Chaudun, the Parisian chocolatier, has noted that sugar is to chocolate what salt is to other foods: a little

enhances the flavor, but too much destroys it. One of the major problems with sugar is that it has insidiously become part of the food-processing industry. Offering little nutritional benefit, sugar is not always used as a sweetener, but rather to improve the overall "mouthfeel" of certain foods.

Another ingredient that has been used in chocolate since Cortés introduced the drink to the Spanish court is vanilla. It is still used by the best manufacturers; although the majority of producers have been using the artificial flavoring ethyl vanillin—derived from certain species of conifer—since its discovery at the beginning of the twentieth century. Vanillin is produced as a by-product of the paper industry and can never replace the complex mix of thousands of chemical elements that create the flavor of a real vanilla pod.

The only other ingredient found in most eating chocolate today is soy lecithin, which acts as an emulsifier and stabilizer and is added at the conching stage. Its main function is to improve the texture and keeping qualities of the chocolate. Recently, however, many fine chocolate manufacturers have been reconsidering this position and removing lecithin from their recipes, as it is considered to be detrimental to the overall flavor.

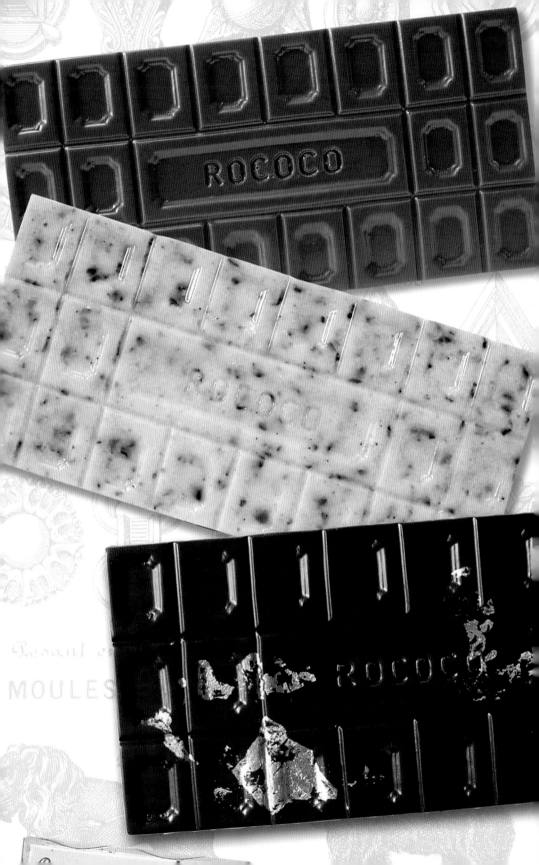

CHOCOLATE STYLES

So far our discussion has concentrated on dark chocolate, because I feel that for the connoisseur it should play a major role in any selection of really fine chocolate. Of course, there is much more to chocolate than bars of milk or dark chocolate, and in this section I will also look at different styles, from the dark chocolate carré to the ultra-sweet cream or fondant. Dark eating chocolate itself comes in an array of styles, mainly characterized by cocoa content, that can vary from the highly astringent and often unpalatable 90 to 100 percent cocoa down to unspeakably sugary "sweet" chocolate with a mere 15 percent. As has been stated, however, it is the quality of beans used that is vital. If we make a comparison with coffee, it does not follow that if you put 10 spoonfuls in the pot, you will get a better flavor. What you want is more flavor, not necessarily more coffee. For this reason, I place Valrhona's Grand Cru chocolates at the top of any list of dark chocolates. Neat marketing ploy that the name may be, it is the standard other chocolate makers aspire to.

PLAIN CHOCOLATE

GRAND CRU

This term was coined by the French company Valrhona in 1986 for their Guanaja plain chocolate couverture, which uses only South American beans. They later developed a Caribbean trinitario chocolate (Pur Caraïbe) and a pure criollo bean chocolate from Madagascar (Manjari). There are also some milk Grand Crus, although I feel that these are better seen as blends of rare cocoa. *Cacaos fins* is the French definition of fine beans such as the trinitario and the criollo. The term Grand Cru is still no absolute guarantee of quality—so beware of cheap imitations, especially in France. In my experience, price was the only similarity.

FINE CHOCOLATE

Since this book was first published in 1995, the chocolate world has moved on a great deal. New chocolate makers have sprung up around the world, producing their own high-quality chocolate from beans following Valrhona's lead. To raise awareness of the new interest in higher quality chocolate, the Academy of Chocolate was formed in the United Kingdom in 2004.

In order to distinguish between high sugar, low cocoa content industrial chocolate, and chocolate made with care from good quality beans, the Academy has come up with a definition of what it considers to be real chocolate. "Fine chocolate" is chocolate with at least 60 percent cocoa solids for dark or 30 percent for milk, with no added vegetable fat and no artificial preservatives or additives. The emulsifier lecithin is allowed, as is real vanilla. Vanillin and "vanilla flavor" are not permitted.

SINGLE ORIGIN

Since Valrhona first produced their Grand Cru chocolate, the idea of "single" or "unique origin" has really caught on. Many chocolate makers, both old and new, have produced chocolate bars where the beans have been sourced from a single country, variety, or even plantation. This has allowed chocolate fans to sample a wealth of flavors and start to think of chocolate as being rather like wine, instead of just a single flavor. Watch out, though, for the many companies now jumping on the bandwagon who buy standard origin couverture from one of the big producers such as Barry Callebaut, then give the impression that they have produced their own origin chocolate from beans.

BRUT (FDA BITTER)

In the United States, the FDA (Food and Drug Administration) describes this as chocolate that does not contain sugar, though it may contain natural or artificial flavoring. Only real fanatics will enjoy eating this since it is usually intended for cooking. I would place any chocolate with a cocoa solid content in excess of 85 percent in this category, as it is likely to be equally unpalatable.

EXTRA AMER

This is my own category for chocolate with 75 to 85 percent cocoa. This is the upper range for what I would consider palatable.

AMER

Again, this is my own category for anything between 50 and 70 percent. All the Grand Crus fall into this category. Much lower than this, and the sweetness will become overbearing.

BITTERSWEET (FDA 35%+)

Unless you are tasting a bittersweet chocolate that has substantially higher than the minimum permitted cocoa content, whatever beans are used will be unlikely to make much impression through the sweetness of this chocolate.

SEMISWEET

This term is used in the United States, but I have not come across any FDA classification of it. At midway between bittersweet and sweet, it has approximately the cocoa content of Nestlé Toll House semi-sweet morsels, widely popular in the United States for baking chocolate chip cookies.

SWEET (FDA 15%+)

I am always amazed when I hear of bars that are made with such a low percentage of cocoa, since this should be the main ingredient. I wonder what else the manufacturers put in. Usually, dark chocolate consists of the cocoa solids, with sugar making up the balance of the ingredients. Valrhona's Manjari, for example, contains 64.5 percent cocoa and 35 percent sugar.

COUVERTURE

Couverture is the French term for the chocolate used by chocolatiers and pastry chefs as one of their raw materials. The direct translation of couverture is covering, which is ironic, as in the English-speaking world the word is synonymous with the lowest-grade waxy cake and cookie (chocolate-flavored) coating. In reality, the cocoa content of cake covering is so low that it bears no comparison with couverture. The French definition of couverture is chocolate containing a minimum of 31 percent cocoa butter—roughly twice the amount found in ordinary eating chocolate. Chocolatiers and pastry chefs choose

Tasting samples of couverture.

to use couverture in order to achieve a high gloss when tempering chocolate, for its ready melting qualities and its workability.

In general it is not easy to find couverture in grocery stores or supermarkets, as it tends to be used only by professionals. However, if you enjoy cooking with chocolate or want to try making your own, it is essential to find a good source of supply. In my opinion, the finest manufacturer of couverture is the French company Valrhona, but many fine chocolate makers favor Barry Callebaut (Belgium), Max Felchlin (Switzerland), or one of the new breed of chocolate makers such as Amedei or Domori from Italy, or Pralus or Chocolaterie de l'Opéra from France. Some chocolatiers even make their own chocolate from cocoa beans.

Choosing a couverture is a very personal matter, and the selection available from different manufacturers is almost unlimited. Personally I favor couvertures made with fine or flavor beans (not too highly roasted), natural vanilla, and ones that have been conched for as long as possible in order to remove any residual astringency.

MILK CHOCOLATE

Milk chocolate most closely reflects each individual country's chocolate tastes. It has always been a specialty of the Swiss, who invented it, and who still produce some of the world's finest milk chocolate. Milk chocolate has less of dark chocolate's subtlety, and the blending of the beans does not have to be such a precise procedure.

There are two main types of milk chocolate, depending on what sort of milk product is used. On the continent of Europe, most manufacturers use condensed milk following the original choice of Peter and Nestlé; while most manufacturers in the United Kingdom and North America use a milk crumb mixture of milk and sugar that has been allowed to dry out on its own, rather than by hot air currents. The distinctive taste of Hershey's milk chocolate, which is known as "barnyard" or "cheesy," is the result of enzyme activity in the milk crumb while it is drying.

Below is a brief summary of the styles of some of the major producers. In good milk chocolate, we should be looking for cocoa flavor, how well the milk offsets the beans, and whether it melts readily in the mouth without leaving any greasy residues.

Belgian milk chocolate tends to be blander and sweeter than Swiss milk chocolate. A recent tasting of a Côte d'Or milk bar was, to use the American terminology, almost "barnyardy." In France, Valrhona have set new standards with their milk chocolate bars and couverture. Maître chocolatier, Pierre Hermé, describes Valrhona's Jivara Lactée as a perfectly honed chocolate that will enable those secret milk chocolate lovers to finally come out of the closet! The archetypal taste in Britain is Cadbury's, which uses the milk crumb method of production. While not having the cheesy Hershey flavor, the best-selling "Dairy Milk" bar has a greasy mouthfeel combined with cloying sweetness. In Switzerland, Lindt, Suchard, Nestlé, and Tobler are world famous producers, but as a result of multinational politics, Lindt is the only one of these giants that is still solely dedicated to chocolate. With relatively few areas of quality bean production left in the world, I wonder whether these producers are still using the criollo bean in their milk chocolate. Swiss milk chocolate was once famed for its aromatic flavor, but compared to Valrhona's Jivara Lactée—with the exception of Lindt—the Swiss milk chocolate I have tasted recently has not been so interesting. In the United States, Hershey is considered to be representative of the American taste. Another U.S. chocolate company is Ghirardelli—better known for its dark chocolate, because its milk is very sweet and a little waxy. Since the first edition of this book I am delighted to say that Scharffenberger has come to challenge the United States by following the European tradition of chocolate making.

WHITE CHOCOLATE

This is a combination of cocoa butter, sugar, and milk, and it is even harder to tell good from bad. Again, watch out for greasiness in the mouth, overbearing sweetness, and a good clean break. Personally, I find it difficult to enjoy white chocolate apart from a few rare exceptions—for example, when it is used for dipping fruit such as strawberries or cape gooseberries (Physalis). In this context, the chocolate balances the acidity of the fruit perfectly; it also marries surprisingly well with spice—especially cardamom and nutmeg.

ORGANIC CHOCOLATE

Pesticides and fertilizers are in general use in large-scale cocoa production as in any other type of intensive farming, but the main worry for plantation owners are fungi, which proliferate in damp tropical climates. The best protection is the creation of hardy hybrids, but this does not lead to beans with a good flavor. This is why, at the moment, organic chocolate is often made from hardy but inferior-tasting beans. In Britain, Green and Black's have become synonymous with organic chocolate. This fast-growing company has been wholly owned by Cadbury's as of 2006. The chocolate—previously made in France—is now produced in Italy by an industrial chocolate manufacturer.

Plantations such as the Los Anconès plantation in the Dominican Republic have shown that it is possible to grow and ship the highest quality beans organically. Their beans are used by Michel Cluizel to make a very fine plantation chocolate, though Cluizel has opted not to certify the final product as organic.

Recently, Valrhona have created one of the first certified organic chocolate bars of a quality near to the best fine chocolate: "Cao Grande" dark and milk bars. The chocolate is made from a blend of beans from Peru and Madagascar, and is available as couverture for chocolatiers to use. We can therefore expect to see some high-quality organic chocolates on the market soon.

FAIR TRADE

As consumers have become increasingly aware of the conditions in which the raw commodities in their food are grown, Fair Trade goods have become more and more popular. Green and Black's have one bar in their range that is Fair Trade, Maya Gold, which was the first ever Fair Trade product; though sadly now this contains only 50 percent cocoa solids, instead of the original 70 percent. Meanwhile, U.K. companies such as The Day Chocolate Company, with its Divine chocolate, and others around the world have made Fair Trade a popular choice for concerned chocolate lovers.

Fair Trade is about setting a fair price for basic commodities. If there is a downfall when it comes to the world of chocolate, the problem with Fair Trade is that it sets a blanket price for all cocoa, regardless of the quality. Fine chocolate makers will almost always pay above the Fair Trade price for their premium beans—sometimes as much as three times the amount. So there is hardly an incentive to adopt Fair Trade, especially given the potential costs involved in the approval process.

Fine chocolate makers usually have direct relations with the plantations on which their cocoa is grown, so are much more accountable than the big companies who mostly buy their cocoa anonymously on the commodity markets. Finally, Fair Trade only creates a higher price for the commodity, cocoa. This means that still only a small fraction of the final price of a chocolate bar goes to the people who grew the pods.

Perhaps the way forward is shown by companies like the Grenada Chocolate Company. Probably the only chocolate company in the world to be based on a plantation, it produces organic chocolate in a local co-operative. There is also Malagasy, an "Equitable Trade" project to produce finished chocolate bars in the country of cocoa production—in this case Madagascar—yet with some of the best cocoa beans.

FILLINGS

We move on now to the different styles you are likely to find in a box of chocolates. This list is not exhaustive because chocolatiers are endlessly inventive. However, most top-quality selections will usually produce a variety that includes many of these categories.

BOILINGS

These centers include caramels, butterscotch, and fudge, and are based on sugar and glucose. Butter and other milk products provide the textural variation, while the temperature at which the mixture is boiled accounts for the softness or hardness of the final product. These are popular in the United Kingdom, the United States, and even Belgium.

CREAMS AND FONDANTS

These are made with sugar, water, and confectionery glucose, and consist of sugar crystals in a sugar syrup that often incorporates fruit and other flavorings. It is then coated in a tempered chocolate.

CROQUANT

This term literally means "crunchy" and refers to molten sugar with the addition of crushed almonds or filberts, depending on the country. It is always a shame when peanuts are substituted—a common practice in the United States, where the confection is known as nut brittle. The best croquant I have eaten, Croccante Gentile, is made by the Italian company Caffarel in Turin.

GIANDUJA

This is very finely ground almonds, filberts, or walnuts, and sugar, mixed with dark or milk chocolate. It is often presented in small, rounded triangular blocks wrapped in foil.

MARZIPAN

This is molten sugar mixed with finely ground almonds—often flavored with pistachios. It is usually coated in tempered chocolate.

PRALINE

This is very similar to a gianduja except that it is usually coated in milk or dark chocolate. Praline was so popular in Belgium that it became the generic term for a particular type of Belgian chocolate characterized by its sweet, whipped creamy center.

NOUGAT

This is also known as *montélimar*, after the French town famous for its manufacture, *torrone* in Italy, and *turrón* in Spain. It is a mixture of whipped egg white, boiled sugar or honey, nuts, and candied fruit.

TRUFFLES, PALETS, AND GANACHES

These provide, for me, the ultimate way of expressing the quality of dark chocolate; making the flavors of the chocolate burst out. A ganache is a mixture of chocolate and cream, usually with some butter added. It may be rolled in cocoa powder, powdered sugar, or finely chopped nuts to create a simple truffle, but normally it will be dipped or enrobed in a coating of tempered chocolate. The palet, or palet d'or, is like a flat version of this. One way of coating is to dip a circle or square of ganache into tempered chocolate, then flip it on to a marble slab covered with flecks of gold leaf to leave the characteristic two or three lines across the bottom of the chocolate. The real skill with truffles and palets is in making a light chocolatey ganache whose flavor offsets or combines well with the coating chocolate.

THE APPRECIATION OF CHOCOLATE

On first opening a bar or box, check that there is a good chocolatey aroma. It should not have any hint of chemicals, coconut, or overwhelming sweetness and certainly must not smell dusty since this indicates that it is either too old or has been badly stored. I feel that it should also not smell too strongly of nuts, even if there are pralines in the selection. Next, we should examine the chocolate. Check the color. It may vary from a deep auburn to the darkest of browns. The finish will depend on whether the chocolates have been molded or enrobed / hand-dipped. In the first case, they will be glossy; otherwise, they have a deep luster. Sometimes acetate film is laid over the dipped chocolate, and when it is peeled off, it leaves a glossy finish.

TASTING

When it comes to tasting the chocolate, it is best to let a small piece gently melt on your tongue. Unless it is a particularly revolting sample, chocolate tasters do not spit out chocolate because information can be gleaned from the "mouthfeel." Is it greasy or waxy? Is there any grittiness? On the negative side, one should check for any smoked or burnt flavors and that it is not too sweet. Is there a good balance between sweet and bitter? Is the use of vanilla subtle or is it overpoweringly artificial? How acidic or astringent is the chocolate? Finally, we should look for a good, long finish, as with a fine wine. If tasting several bars, take a sip of water between the different samples, or you can freshen the palate with a piece of apple. Although coffee goes well with chocolate, it dulls the palate in the same way as other strong flavors such as chili or peppermint, so is to be avoided at serious tastings.

Professional tasters often use the same vocabulary as the wine trade. Different "notes" or characteristics are looked for, and compared with fruits, flower blossoms, balsam, and even green tea. Certain bean varieties have unusual characteristic flavors, though you will be very fortunate to come across a bar of chocolate with such a flavor.

SNAP

If it is a bar of chocolate that you are tasting, break it and listen to check that it snaps cleanly. The crystalline structure of cocoa butter gives the characteristic crisp snap. It should be a good clean break and should not shatter everywhere. If it is a bonbon, you will be able to see if the chocolate has a thick or thin coat or if it has been double or triple-coated. The current trend

Fine chocolate should snap cleanly.

When tasting chocolate, it is important to look out for "bloom."

in the finest French chocolates is for a fine layer of chocolate to be added to the ganache or praline before it is enrobed. If you hold the chocolate for a few seconds, it should begin to melt—unless it contains lots of vegetable fats or your circulation is particularly bad!

BLOOM

"Bloom" is the term for the grayish-white appearance sometimes seen on the surface of chocolate. It resembles the white surface sometimes seen on plums and other soft fruit, though the cause is very different in chocolate. There are two types of bloom which can develop. The first is caused by cocoa butter and indicates that the chocolate has become too warm at some point. This makes the cocoa butter crystals rise to the surface, and, on cooling, they recrystallize. The taste is unaffected, and if necessary or appropriate, the problem can be resolved by retempering.

Much more serious is sugar bloom, which occurs when moisture comes into contact with the chocolate. This will typically happen in a refrigerator. The sugar crystals are drawn to the surface and dissolve in the water vapor, later recrystallizing. The process destroys the texture of the chocolate, which becomes gray and gritty and, although edible, will hardly delight the connoisseur.

STORING AND SERVING

To keep chocolate in its optimum condition, it is necessary to keep it away from light, moisture, and foreign odors in a room with a maximum relative humidity of 65 percent. The temperature should be 54°F (12°C) to 64°F (18°C). Good dark chocolate should keep for at least 1½ years without losing quality in these conditions, and can be eaten long after that. White and milk chocolate will not keep for as long, but they are surprisingly robust.

As far as fresh truffles or other chocolates made with cream are concerned, they are eaten ideally within a few hours. In tasting for this book, it became obvious that there is an enormous difference between a ganache which is a day or two old and one that has been kept waiting for two weeks. Truffles that have been made with genuinely fresh cream and little sugar may start to turn moldy after a week, especially if any air pockets have crept in between ganache and coating. The use of a little invert sugar (a product that is chemically close to honey and also helps prevent crystallization) and long-life cream will extend the shelf life to about two weeks.

There is never any need to keep chocolate in the refrigerator when you have a cool room available. It is, however, possible to store chocolate in the freezer or fridge, but it must be in an airtight container which has also been wrapped to prevent any moisture from accumulating. You should always bring chocolates back up to room temperature before opening the package.

Good presentation really enhances the chocolate experience.

STAR RATINGS

Each chocolatier has been given one of the following star ratings:

★   high street quality

★ ★   average to good quality

★ ★ ★   good to excellent quality

★ ★ ★ ★   the very best quality available

★ ★ ★ ★ ★   a master chocolatier

CHOCOLATIERS

THE
CHOCOLATE
DIRECTORY

ALTMANN & KÜHNE
★ ★ ★

Graben 30, A-1010 Vienna, Austria
Tel: (43-1) 533 09 27 Fax: (43-1) 216 54 02
www.feinspitz.com/ak

Altmann & Kühne was established more than 90 years ago by Emil Altmann, and since the first shop opened, the burghers of Vienna have beaten a path to their door. At one time there were three shops, but today there remains just one—situated near St. Stephen's Cathedral in the center of Vienna.

The current maître chocolatier, 42-year-old Leopold Eggenberger, often starts work in the dead of night, making the confections that will later be dipped in chocolate by a team of 15 women. The work is painstaking, as each chocolate is a perfect miniature bonbon that is shaped, then chocolate-dipped, entirely by hand, and finished with tiny gold and silver balls, perfect whole pistachios and filberts, or with a swirl. The recipes have remained unchanged since the first shop opened, and no preservatives are used. The packaging is designed by the current owner, Petra Heytmanek-Schick, whose parents own one of the great Austrian hotel dynasties. To receive a miniature chest of drawers filled with exquisite doll's house-sized chocolates must be every child's dream come true.

🍫 TASTING NOTES 🍫

These exquisitely made, doll's house-sized chocolates, carefully packed in white cups and tissue, arrived in perfect condition.

MINIATURE CHOCOLATE HEART: filled with a very smooth, sweet, and vanilla-laden gianduja.

TINY ROUND CHOCOLATES: these were topped with silver or gold balls, and filled with a crunchy hazelnut and coffee croquant.

PINK FRUIT FONDANT: this was very tangy and surprisingly good—perfect for fondant lovers.

SPICY ORANGE GINGERBREAD: this fairy-tale confection was coated with white sugar balls.

HOUSE SPECIALTIES: miniature chocolates, nougat with rum, fondants, grains de café, and seasonal specialties.

COUVERTURES USED: Suchard and Knäbchen.

AMEDEI
★ ★ ★ ★

Via San Gervasio 29, 56020 La Rotta (Pontedera), Pisa, Italy
Tel: (39-587) 484 849 Fax: (39-587) 483 208
www.amedei.it

In the early 1990s, the young Alessio and Cecilia Tessieri grew frustrated with their efforts to obtain couverture from Valrhona for their budding praline business. Luckily for the world of fine chocolate, this inspired them to begin producing their own chocolate. When an Italian producer in the Tuscan "chocolate valley" closed down, the brother and sister team were able to buy the traditional machinery. With the help of one of the chocolate makers from the old factory, Alessio and Cecilia learnt how to use the machinery, and by 1993 were producing their very first "Toscano Black" chocolate in a converted iron foundry in Pontedera—not too far from Pisa in the Tuscan hills. This was only the beginning, however: Alessio began to travel the world looking for cocoa beans; while Cecilia became a master chocolate maker—she is probably the only female fine chocolate maker in the world. By 1998 they were beginning to perfect the recipe that would earn them their worldwide reputation.

At first, Amedei bought the beans to make their chocolate from traders in Europe. Then, after visiting Venezuela, they began to experiment with the beans they had brought back to Tuscany. The results seemed superior, and the Tessieris soon realized that cocoa beans must be grown with care, and properly fermented and dried, in order to produce the best chocolate. They developed direct relations with plantations, helping cocoa growers to improve the quality of their

crops; and paid a higher price for the beans. They sought out the finest bean varieties and plantations. Realizing that the legendary Chuao region on the Venezuelan coast had some of the best stock, Amedei negotiated an exclusive deal with this historic village and plantation, also called Chuao. These days, Amedei's chocolate from Chuao beans is recognized as one of the best in the world, and has been a double gold winner at the Academy of Chocolate awards.

Amedei continues to expand its range of chocolate—always seeking to improve—and has now developed an extensive range of Italian-style pralines and truffles using its own couverture. Even so, its strength unquestionably still lies in chocolate making.

❦ TASTING NOTES ❦

With flavors ranging from hazelnut to Grappa, Amedei have a good array of Mediterranean-influenced truffles. Their secret weapon, however, is undoubtedly their chocolate, which is widely recognized to be some of the best in the world and a benchmark for others.

PRALINES AND BONBONS: there was a good assortment of Italian-style chocolates, many with a nut base. The traditional combination of sugar and nuts acts as a natural preservative, and many of the well-known Italian specialties such as gianduja have come about because of this natural long-life combination.

CARAMELS AND GANACHES: Amedei have worked hard to achieve careful flavor balances here, but (as is the Italian style) these were rather sweet.

HOUSE SPECIALTIES: the famed Chuao and Porcelana chocolate.

COUVERTURES USED: their own.

ANGELINA
✦ ✦ ✦

226 Rue de Rivoli, 75001 Paris, France
Tel: (33-1) 42 60 82 00 Fax: (33-1) 42 86 98 97

R umpelmayer's family business was founded in Nice in 1870 by Austrian-born Antoine Rumpelmayer. The empire expanded to Paris in 1903. It was Antoine's son René, however, who created the legend of Angelina (his wife's name). Located opposite the Tuileries Gardens in Paris, this famous chocolate house has been a meeting point for Parisian society since 1903: after René's death, Angelina received King George V of England; and Marcel Proust and Madame Coco Chanel frequently took tea at this fashionable watering hole.

Even with large premises on the Rue de Rivoli, there is still often a line here for tables. Morning coffee and chocolate are served, as well as light lunches and sumptuous teas. Most famous of all are the jugs of thick, rich Chocolat à l'Africain, which come with bowls of cold whipped cream. This drink is also sold in packets, so that you can make it at home—though it would be hard to recreate the period atmosphere found inside Angelina.

❦ TASTING NOTES ❦

A good selection of pralines, marzipans, and ganache centers, which draw from the French, Austrian, and Swiss traditions.

PISTACHIO MARZIPAN: this had a good texture.

OBLONG PALET: this flat-topped chocolate revealed a sandwich of very good almond marzipan and a smooth rum truffle.

LOZENGE WITH LEMON GANACHE: the chocolate was very smooth and contained bits of lemon zest—a refreshing combination.

ROCHER: coated with almond chips, this was filled with a rich and slightly grainy praline.

DARK PRALINE: this had a crumbly center, and good, rich, well-balanced chocolate.

HOUSE SPECIALTIES: hot chocolate, tins of caramels, and bonbons.

COUVERTURES USED: top secret.

AUX DÉLICES DE LA TOUR
✦ ✦ ✦

1 Rue des Lices, Angers, France
Tel: (33-2) 41 88 9452

F ounded in 1975 in the heart of the historic French town of Angers, this very small artisan business employs just five people.

Gilbert Benoit, the 58-year-old maître chocolatier, opened the shop in Angers after running a successful boulangerie, pâtisserie, and confiserie shop in the Nantes region. Throughout his professional career, while continuing to attend courses at the Ecole LeNôtre in Paris, Benoit's maxim has been to use nothing but fresh, high-quality products, and he is continually trying to find new recipes.

Madame Benoit is relied upon to display her husband's chocolates tastefully in the shop's five windows. Tasteful, too, is the packaging of the chocolates in a small, dark brown box with a shiny gold ribbon: simple but elegant.

❦ TASTING NOTES ❦

The chocolates have Robert Linxe-style flat tops, and a very thin, crisp, fine coating of chocolate.

RECTANGULAR, MARBLED GANACHE: this had real body with a delicate, fresh, vanilla flavor, added butter, and a good, long finish.

LE PLANTAGENET: this dark palet was a delicate ganache, made with Cointreau, and filled with crunchy chopped almonds.

CRUNCHY PRALINE PALET SQUARE: this was made with good white chocolate that was not too sweet.

WHITE CHOCOLATE WITH POWDERED SUGAR: this had an inside layer of marzipan, surrounding a ganache, and was the least favorite in the box.

HOUSE SPECIALTIES: le Marbre Amer, les Coquineries du Roi René, les truffes Angevines au Cointreau, and le Plantagenet; as well as molded clogs and seasonal specialties, such as St. Nicholas figurines.

COUVERTURES USED: Chocolaterie du Pecq.

BAIXAS
★ ★ ★ ★ ★

Calaf 9-11, 08021 Barcelona, Spain
Tel: (34-3) 209 25 42 Fax: (34-3) 414 49 84

Without a doubt, one of Spain's finest producers of "designer" chocolate, Baixas commissioned the artist José-Maria Trias to make a series of boxes based on the architectural, cubist, and surrealist themes that are so influential in Barcelona. Tributes to Salvador Dali and Gaudi abound and form the basis of this series of 15 highly collectable boxes, produced between 1971 and 1991.

Baixas was founded in 1958 as a pâtisserie by Francisco Baixas and his wife Conxita, and by 1968 had added chocolate making to its repertoire, with the help of chef chocolatier Eugenio Aguilar. Aguilar has continued to be "the right hand" in the chocolate production. In 1982 Francisco's son, Joan, joined the team after training extensively in Europe. Joan worked with Fauchon in Paris and Wittamer in Brussels, among others; becoming a member of the International Association of Relais Desserts in 1985. Two years later, his sister Nuria took over as traiteur of the newly inaugurated Salon de Thé restaurant in the Calaf area of Barcelona.

Sadly, in the same year Francisco died, but not before seeing his dream of the Salon de Thé realized, and his children continuing the tradition of fine quality and excellent service.

❦ TASTING NOTES ❦

This was an interesting selection, with nature-inspired shapes and unexpected, refreshing combinations.

FLEUR DE LYS: hand-piped in rich, dark chocolate, this concealed four freshly roasted, crunchy golden filberts—very good.

CHESTNUT: this rich, fruity dark chocolate was filled with a light, buttery, raspberry ganache.

MAPLE LEAF: this was filled with a pale green buttercream center, made with fresh mint. It was a smooth, delicate, light, and refreshing combination, and delightfully unsweet.

DARK LOG WITH MILK STRIPES: this was a very sweet whipped rum truffle.

HOUSE SPECIALTIES: Neapolitans, giandujas, fresh buttercream chocolates, Tea Timers chocolate bars topped with whole almonds, and almond and filbert chocolates. Seasonal specialties include Christmas turrón and Easter fantasy creations.

COUVERTURES USED: Valrhona, Callebaut, Cocoa Cream Caracas, and Guayaquil.

BARATTI & MILANO

★ ★ ★

Piazza Castello, 27, 10123 Turin, Italy
Tel: (39-11) 561 30 60 Fax: (39-11) 561 26 66

A relative newcomer to gianduja production, this house was founded in Turin in 1858 by Ferdinando Baratti and Eduardo Milano. In 1875, the Lord Mayor officiated at a presentation of the Royal Family's coat of arms, which Baratti & Milano have used ever since on their logo. The shop drew huge crowds, and one attraction was the huge mirror—apparently the largest in Italy. This master chocolatier was also a focal point for many artists, politicians, scientists, and writers of the time; including a prominent doctor who helped to increase sales by recommending consumption of the shop's chocolates for their restorative qualities!

Baratti & Milano's café continues to thrive in the elegant surrounds of the Piazza Castello, in the heart of Turin. The company's motto, "Our quality makes history," remains as true as ever.

BÉLINE
✫ ✫ ✫

5 Place Saint-Nicolas, 72000 Le Mans, France
Tel: (33-2) 43 28 00 43 Fax: (33-2) 43 87 62 85
www.jacques-bellanger-chocolatier.com

In 1977 Eugène Béline set up his chocolate production à l'ancienne, using old recipes and methods that adhered strictly to a fine gourmet tradition. Since 1995, the business has been owned by Jacques Bellanger, who gained official recognition as one of the "meilleurs ouvriers de France"—an accolade awarded only to the finest artisans in France.

🍫 TASTING NOTES 🍫

This was a varied selection, ranging from rather ordinary dark chocolate, crunchy, almond praline to surprisingly good milk chocolate and strong coffee ganache.

DARK CHOCOLATE OBLONG: this was a fragrant lemon ganache, with little bits of lemon peel.

DARK CHOCOLATE SQUARES: the palet with gold leaf was filled with a strong vanilla ganache; another had a dark fruity ganache that initially could have been apricot or citrus fruit, but was, in fact, raspberry, which came through at the end; the square decorated with a plastic leaf was rich and smooth with rum or calvados; and the crunchy nuts and fennel aroma of another made a successful combination.

ROUND DARK CHOCOLATES: one filled with a rough almond and orange peel marzipan was very festive; and the coffee cream was a good Irish coffee—very like the drink.

HOUSE SPECIALTIES: Bugattises—chocolate with praline and caramelized sugar; Les Paves du Vieux Mans—creamy coffee ganache; Les Coeurs de la Reine Berangère—praline and filbert cream; Le Schubert—ganache and almond in Cointreau flavor; Les Mancelles—surfine praline and roasted filbert and cacao; Les Rillettes—a special recipe of chocolate with orange and praline flavor—the chocolate version of a rich potted meat spread.

COUVERTURES USED: Callebaut.

BERNACHON
★ ★ ★ ★ ★

42 Cours Franklin Roosevelt, 69006 Lyon, France
Tel: (33-4) 78 24 37 98 Fax: (33-4) 78 52 67 77
www.bernachon.com

Deeply rooted in the great culinary traditions of Lyon, the acclaimed center of the gastronomic world, the Bernachon family have come to represent the last great chocolate dynasty. At the age of 14, Maurice ("Papa") Bernachon was sent to be an apprentice pâtissier under the direction of Monsieur Debeauge in Pont de Beauvoisin. At the time, chocolate was a rare commodity; only affordable to the very richest families.

The atelier was established in 1955 behind the shop in the Cours Franklin Roosevelt, and remains little changed to this day. It would be unthinkable today to set up such an enterprise—with each part of the production, from the roasting of the cocoa beans to the dipping of truffles, taking place right in the heart of the most fashionable quarter in Lyon. Until recently, the Bernachons housed their employees in dormitories above the workshops, and even today the company dining rooms feed all 50 artisan chocolatiers.

Behind the glittering series of three shops is a labyrinthine network of rooms; the heady scent of chocolate is almost overwhelming, and there is something tropical about the aroma—a ripeness and volatility. Bernachon et Fils have preserved an almost extinct genre of chocolate making: at the turn of the century, there were approximately 100 artisan chocolate producers in France; now it seems they can be counted on the fingers of one hand. The most striking thing about the Bernachon enterprise is that although father and son are so fervent about the tradition they preserve, they are also so generous in spirit. They hide nothing—not even their trade secret—from visitors to the atelier, and the provenance of the beans is clearly marked on the sacks of beans. There is an integrity found so rarely in the chocolate business these days. A passion and dedication, a wisdom, and clarity of vision have sustained the business. The Bernachons have resisted the temptation to expand because they believe this would compromise the one thing that is not negotiable: the quality of their chocolate. They remain convinced that expansion could never succeed for these reasons—everything depends on the unity of the family business, and the abiding presence of real masters.

BERNACHON
★ ★ ★ ★ ★

It is almost unheard of today for a chocolatier to start with a cocoa bean and finish with a chocolate truffle or bonbon. It equates to a baker milling his own wheat or a chef butchering his own meat. Almost without exception, master chocolate makers source the chocolate couverture as a raw material and from there proceed to create their own confections. The Bernachons have traveled the world in search of the finest cocoa plantations, the rarest cocoa bean varieties, and most importantly, the best terroir: that "right" soil to grow that elusive perfectly flavored bean.

In the final assessment, as with wine, the soil is the deciding factor, with sunshine and humidity also crucial. The very best beans come from Latin America, Sri Lanka, and Madagascar. Mainland Africa, although it produces the largest volume of cocoa in the world, is of little interest to such connoisseurs, as the soil is poor, and in general it is planted with inferior varieties of cocoa.

Around 19.7 tons of cocoa beans are used each year in the manufacture of Bernachon's different cuvées, selected from the finest plantations in the world, and shipped via

❧ TASTING NOTES ❧

The truffles, pralines, giandujas, and marzipans were exceptionally good; and all the nutty ones were fresh and crunchy. Rich dark chocolate dominated the selection.

PRINCESS: green pistachio marzipan covered a large, Grand Marnier-filled center.

AMANDE-PRINCESS: wrapped in green foil, this crunchy croquant of almond brittle with a gooey almond praline on top was enrobed in dark chocolate. It was very good as it had lots of toffee, but did not stick to the teeth.

PALET D'OR: very rich and fruity without the bitterness of the extra amer, this was delicious— as good as the truffle.

CARAMEL: before putting the flat square— halfway to being a toffee—in the mouth, the chocolate aroma was very strong, but the buttery caramel dominated in the mouth. It was unctuous and fantastic.

MONTÉLIMAR: a bit bland but very well made, this was not too chewy.

GUITAR / LANGUE DE CHAT: this brittle croquant, with lumps of nut, was similar to Gold Cup, but crunchier and more chocolatey.

PRALINE WITH AN ORANGE FRAGRANCE: a slightly pitted cross-section revealed finely shaved orange peel that was steeped in syrup. The chocolate was very well balanced and not too sweet.

OVAL "ROCOCO" MOLDED SHELL: filled with a smooth, fragrant, delicate green paste made from pistachios, this had, perhaps, a little white rum added. It was good and moist.

HOUSE SPECIALTIES: Truffle Maison, le Palet d'Or, chocolate cake Président, chocolate bars, and seasonal specialties at Easter.

COUVERTURES USED: these are all made on the premises from specially selected fine beans from around the world. Only pure Madagascan vanilla is used. No lecithin is added. The blocks of couverture are aged in a special cool room for three months.

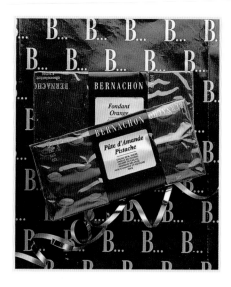

BERNACHON

★ ★ ★ ★ ★

Bordeaux. When they arrive at Bernachon, the beans are roasted gently for about 20 minutes to remove any residual traces of humidity. After this they are tasted and, if necessary, roasted a little longer to bring out the optimum flavor. Beans of this quality need to be treated with great respect; over-roasting would result in burnt and bitter flavors normally associated with inferior beans.

The beans are then nibbed and ground; extra cocoa butter, pure Bourbon vanilla, and sugar are added; and finally the couverture is conched for several days, to refine the texture and remove any traces of astringency. Milk is added to some of the chocolate before the conching stage; however, the chocolates are predominantly dark. White chocolate is almost never used, except in minute quantities as a decorative finish.

With dark couverture of this caliber, it is hardly surprising that white chocolate is not taken seriously. The cocoa beans themselves have such a force: a tropical fruitiness which positively explodes as the finished chocolate melts on the palate. For this reason, the palets

d'or and plain truffles are the most remarkable. Thick Normandy cream is used, together with beurre de Charentes, and these serve as the perfect foil for the rich, aromatic ganache. They use filberts from Piedmont, two different varieties of almonds from Provence, and pistachios from Sicily; and all the fruit confit and peels are made in-house, using whenever possible the freshest local produce. The resulting chocolates are breathtaking and well worth a detour from any corner of the world. Failing that, you could always call and have your order air-freighted to you...

Bernachon refuses to expand beyond the heart of Lyon, feeling that the quality of their product would inevitably be compromised—a refreshing attitude in these times of speculation, takeovers, and mergers. As if to complete the golden circle, Jean Jacques Bernachon married the daughter of one of Lyon's most celebrated chefs: Paul Bocuse. When Maurice Bernachon passed away in 1988, grandchildren Stephanie and Philippe Bernachon took over as the business passed to another generation. Who could possibly compete with such a family?

BERNARD DUFOUX
✫ ✫ ✫ ✫ ✫

32 & 40 Rue Centrale, 71800 La Clayette, Lyon, France
Tel: (33-3) 85 28 08 10 Fax: (33-3) 85 26 83 56
www.chocolatsdufoux.com

Started in 1960, the Bernard Dufoux chocolate shop has grown with the increasing popularity of dark chocolate. Since being voted third-best French chocolatier in 1990 by the Club des Croqueurs, it has been constantly visited by chocolate lovers. Ever obliging maître chocolatier Bernard Dufoux has started to share his professional secrets by doing demonstrations on the first Wednesday or Thursday afternoon of each month. When I visited in 1997, I was delighted to see Bernard at work with a group of young schoolchildren.

❦ TASTING NOTES ❦

The chocolates were excellent: well balanced and full of body, flavor, and aroma; of good texture; and with a long finish.

AMANDE AMERE: tasting of bitter almond essence, this chocolate was fruity and good.

CABRION ORANGE: this orange ganache had good citrus flavor and acidity.

CRIOLLO: this was a layered coffee cream and ganache.

PALAIS BOURBON: this was a very good dark vanilla ganache.

FRAMBOISE: this was a raspberry ganache.

CHOCOPHILE: a mousse with 70 percent cocoa, this could have been a Manjari truffle.

HOUSE SPECIALTIES: masterpieces include a trompe l'oeil fois gras, which is made from chestnuts, studded with chocolate pieces, and laid out on a plate with pistachios, raspberries, and three different sauces—crème Anglaise, a hot chocolate sauce, and raspberry coulis. Other specialties include dark chocolate palet filled with chocolate mousse; Truffino—chocolate mousse with rum-soaked raisins; Malakoff—caramelized almonds; Bigorneau—filbert paste with a base of nougatine; Peche—almond marzipan and peaches; Moustache—almond marzipan with pistachio; Antillais—almond paste and raisins; Togolais—raisins and orange; Caramel—made with salted butter. Other flavors include wild blackberry, fresh mint, autumn raspberry, blackcurrant, and "le Green"—which is made from fresh green leaves according to the season.

COUVERTURES USED: Valrhona with Venezuelan and Caribbean beans.

CACAO SAMPAKA
★ ★ ★

Parc Activitats Economiques, C/Tortosa, 2, 08500 Vic, Spain
Tel: (34-93) 272 08 33 Fax: (34-93) 487 26 23
www.cacaosampaka.com

In 1999, a group of Spanish chocolate professionals felt that the chocolate available in their native Barcelona was either too exclusive and expensive, or at the cheaper end of the market and so just not of good enough quality. Cacao Sampaka was founded to create a happy medium where good quality yet simply packaged chocolates were available in a stylish, accessible shop. With its spacious café area—where customers could enjoy a light meal and thick hot chocolate—the shop soon became a big hit in Barcelona. Five more shops had opened by 2005, along with a bigger factory.

The cornerstone series of eight types of flavors was created by chocolatiers Ramon Morató and Quim Capdevila. These range from traditional flavors to more outlandish combinations with anchovies or olive oil!

🍫 TASTING NOTES 🍫

SINGLE BEAN ORIGIN BOX: this featured dark chocolate from eight different bean countries. Many had an intense bitterness on eating, but this always resolved into a fairly good length. Santo Domingo was robust and fruity, while the Venezuelan was a disappointment, given how good Venezuelan chocolate can be. Costa Rica was light and perfumed, with hints of coffee.

FLOWER AND HERB COLLECTIONS: the thyme in milk chocolate was refreshing and authentic, while the lavender was a little faint.

FRUIT COLLECTION: this was perhaps the least attractive, with odd blocks of color on the chocolates. However, the flavors were generally good, with coconut and pineapple being an unlikely success. The ganaches were mostly of a good quality and not too sweet, even if the presentation was a little basic.

HOUSE SPECIALTIES: chocolate and fruit jam, and a range of chocolate accessories—including utensils, molds, and books.

COUVERTURES USED: Chocovic.

CAFFAREL
✴ ✴

Via Gianevello 41, 10062 Luserna San Giovanni (TO), Italy
Tel: (39-121) 90 03 44 Fax: (39-121) 90 18 53
www.caffarel.com

One of Europe's oldest established chocolate houses, it was Caffarel that inspired the Swiss youth François Louis Cailler to set up the first chocolate factory in Switzerland. Even in the early 1800s, there was much cross-border trade between Italy and Switzerland, and it was at a Swiss village fair that Cailler first smelled the fragrant mixture of chocolate and filberts being made by Caffarel. So enthralled was the young Cailler that he begged to be taken back to Italy to learn the trade of chocolate making. He trained at Caffarel for four years before returning to Switzerland as a maître chocolatier. In 1819, Cailler designed and built a cocoa press complete with stone roller, and he opened the first Swiss chocolate factory at Corsier near Vevey.

The Caffarel factory was opened outside Turin in the early 1800s, situated next to a river which harnessed the water power in order to drive the hydraulic wheel and cocoa mill. The exact dates are a bit hazy, but an early newspaper clipping from around this time confirmed that "Caffarel Father & Son—have purchased from Bozelli of Genoa a machine to make chocolate." Having taken the path leading to industrialization, the company began to grow into a truly modern concern; although it would never set aside the spirit of artisanship that was by now so deeply engrained.

Caffarel invented gianduiotti in 1852. This new variety of chocolate was produced by blending cocoa powder and sugar, with Piedmont's celebrated round and fragrant

filberts. The name came from the word "givu" (in Piedmont dialect), which became "gianduiotto," a nickname destined to win the acclaim of gourmets and gluttons around the world. The process of forcing the chocolate through a pastry bag into molds used to be performed completely by hand, but is now done by a specially designed machine. The result is deceptive, however—the gianduiotti still look as if they have been made by hand.

TASTING NOTES

Caffarel's products are of exemplary quality and are beautifully presented. Best of all are the attractive blue and gold cans, filled with the gianduiotti, and the blue and white tin filled with individually wrapped Croccante Gentile.

GIANDUIOTTI: these are smooth and nutty, melting perfectly in the mouth without a trace of greasiness.

CROCCANTE GENTILE: one of the best croquants made from filberts that you are likely to find.

HOUSE SPECIALTIES: Gianduia 1865; Noblesse, filbert foiled squares; and the box of assorted pralines. Seasonal specialties include red-foiled chocolate roses, hearts, ladybugs, and bumblebees; gold bars and money; and large and small Easter eggs.

COUVERTURES USED: these are made in-house using directly imported cocoa beans, the rarest of them being the Esmeralda from Ecuador and Angoleta from Samoa.

CAMILLE BLOCH
✮ ✮ ✮

Grand-Rue 21, CH-2608 Courtelary, Switzerland
Tel: (41-32) 945 12 00 Fax: (41-32) 945 12 01
www.camillebloch.ch

Camille Bloch started making chocolates in his kitchen at home in Bern in 1929, using ready-made couverture. It was the same year as the Wall Street Crash and marked the start of the worldwide Depression. Four years later, Bloch began to produce chocolate from cocoa beans, in the face of much competition from the old "pioneers," who were, by now, well established. During World War II, there was a great shortage of raw materials, especially cocoa beans, so Camille Bloch put his mind to inventing a new product and, sourcing supplies of almonds and filberts from Turkey and Spain, he created Ragusa—a forerunner of their famous Torino bar—from praline.

Since 1998, the company has been in the hands of the third generation, under Daniel and Stéphane Bloch, who inherited the business from Camille's son, Rolf. Now producing 12 tons of chocolate every day, this company ranks as the fourth-largest chocolate producer in Switzerland. In spite of its size, the company is still run as ordained by Camille Bloch, and the workforce of 150 have a variety of benefits offered to them—from accommodation, health care, and a special company pension to a restaurant and in-house magazine. Camille Bloch is not, however, aiming to become a multinational company. It wants to stay small enough to guarantee daily quality control and keep in close touch with its customers and the market: a refreshing attitude these days!

❦ TASTING NOTES ❦

The chocolates I tasted were fresh, glossy, and much more delicious than I was expecting. They had a strong, possibly artificial, vanilla aroma, with a cool melting sensation in the mouth—reminiscent of the Pyrenéen chocolates of bygone days.

CRUNCHY PRALINE: this was good, with a very fresh toasted filbert on top.

NEAPOLITANS: little and sweet, the flavors were Café, Torino, Zarbitter, and Cric Crac.

HOUSE SPECIALTIES: Neapolitans, liqueurs without the sugar crust, and the seasonal specialties of Kirsch-li, Truffle Buchette, and Ragusa Jubilee.

COUVERTURES USED: they make their own.

CHARBONNEL ET WALKER
✷ ✷

1, The Royal Arcade, 28 Old Bond Street, London W1X 4BT, UK
Tel: (44-20) 7491 0939 Fax: (44-20) 7495 6279
www.charbonnel.co.uk

It was Edward VII who encouraged Madame Charbonnel to leave her Paris chocolate house, Maison Boissier, to join Mrs Walker in London in order to establish one of the earliest fine confectionery houses in England. It opened in London's Mayfair in 1875, and because the shop has always held a Royal Warrant, it has been the victim of many acquisitions and mergers. In 1989, the company returned to private ownership and introduced an innovative selection of chocolate truffle sauces, molinillos, jugs, and drinking chocolate, which keep the same corporate image and packaging style of their established lines.

In some ways the packaging is an outstanding feature of these chocolates, but since Charbonnel's acquisition of the Belgian Maxwell & Kennedy chain, there has been a number of unwelcome changes in the line of chocolates. Although their classic Rose and Violet creams remain some of the finest examples of their genre, anything in a molded shell will almost certainly be a "continental" style filling; an area which I feel is moving away from Charbonnel's fine English tradition. Charbonnel has, however, maintained its tradition of Boîtes Blanches: huge round boxes that contain messages spellt out on foil-wrapped chocolates. Their numbered chocolate system dates back to 1901, which allows customers to pick their own personal selection, ensuring that no unwanted "surprise" centers creep in. Charbonnel has recently grown, taking over another traditional English chocolate company, Ackermans, and perhaps inevitably, has become more commercial.

🍫 TASTING NOTES 🍫

This varied selection included both classics and "continental" style chocolates.

ROSE CREAM: this was an excellent, firm, highly perfumed fondant in good dark chocolate.

STEM GINGER IN DARK CHOCOLATE: the ginger had a crunchy texture, and was strong and slightly hot.

BATON: this looked like it might have been orange peel, but was in fact a very hard and crunchy nougatine coated in dark chocolate.

NUTTY CHOCOLATES: a walnut-topped chocolate contained a walnut ganache of good texture, while a crisp Brazil nut was coated with good dark chocolate.

ALMOND MARZIPAN: this had slight banana notes.

TRUFFLES: these included a whipped vanilla mousse; an artificial-tasting whipped orange; a grainy-textured, whipped, milky filling; and a very sweet bubblegum or possibly, Champagne-flavored whipped truffle in dark chocolate.

HOUSE SPECIALTIES: enrobed coffee beans, Bittermints, Mint Crisps, Mocha Batons, Maple Brazils, Crème Parisiennes, and Chocolate Stem Ginger are all enduring classics; along with a chocolate champagne bottle filled with champagne truffles, and novelties at Christmas and Easter.

COUVERTURES USED: Belgian couverture.

CHARLEMAGNE
✶ ✶

Place Jacques Brel 8, 4040 Herstal, Belgium
Tel: (32-4) 264 66 44 Fax: (32-4) 264 45 18
www.charlemagne.be

Founded in 1974 by Denise Courant-Bellefroid and Jean François Staesbolet, Charlemagne was the product of the unlikely liaison of the tastebuds of an art and culinary historian and the commercial skills of a former endive farmer. Together they developed the concept of "l'autre chocolat," where only natural ingredients of the highest quality and consistency are used—except for vanillin—and no shortcuts are taken.

The name has been taken from the place where Charlemagne was born in the eighth century—also the site of the chocolate production unit today. Charlemagne's royal stamp is imprinted on each chocolate thin. Each confection is created with the help of Denise's fine palate, creativity, and technical expertise.

🍫 TASTING NOTES 🍫

Overall, the added sugar crystals did nothing for the flavor or texture of the chocolates, just making them very sweet.

BLACK WRAPPER: ginger flavored with a citrus tang, this had lots of crunchy sugar.

DUCK EGG BLUE: this spiced ginger, which was very pungent, had a slightly musty flavor.

DARK BLUE: this cinnamon chocolate with crunchy sugar had 46 percent cocoa mass.

WHITE: an orange flower with no extra sugar, this had 60 percent cocoa mass.

RED: this was a very fragrant cardamom and delicate coffee with added crunchy sugar.

GREEN: peppermint with no sugar crystals.

BEIGE: this spiced Earl Grey tea had no sugar crystals and a 54 percent cocoa mass.

HOUSE SPECIALTIES: boxes of thin, flat, squares of chocolate bearing the Charlemagne logo; and a range of flavored organic chocolate bars, made with beans from Belize.

COUVERTURES USED: their own.

CHOCOCO
☆ ☆ ☆

Commercial Road, Swanage, Dorset BH19 1DF, UK
Tel: (44-1929) 421 777
www.chococo.co.uk

Based in the scenic Purbeck peninsular on the south coast of England, Chococo was founded by Andy and Claire Burnet in 2002 when they decided to leave their City jobs in marketing and finance. Seeking a change of lifestyle and a more pleasant location, they relocated to Swanage on the Isle of Purbeck to produce fresh fine chocolates. Besides quality and taste, they have also taken an interest in the source of their ingredients and the ethical consequences of their production. They use fresh Dorset cream in their hand-dipped truffles, and no preservatives. Having built up a local audience for their concoctions, Chococo's reputation has quickly grown beyond the small town of Swanage—with interest from national media and a raft of awards.

Chococo is a family affair, with Andy and Claire's five-year-old daughter, Lily, holding the position of chief taster. Other family members and local friends have become involved, forming an extended clan that turns out all of Chococo's chocolate production by hand; at the same time maintaining a high quality. Chocolates are made fresh to order, as all cream-filled confections must be eaten within two weeks.

British chocolatiers generally have a reputation for oversweet, average quality chocolates that imitate the Belgian style; especially those located outside London. Chococo has really proved that it is possible to produce the highest quality chocolates in a modern style in regional Britain, while respecting local traditions.

CHOCOCO

* * *

🍫 TASTING NOTES 🍫

This was a simple but well-presented selection, featuring a mix of dipped and molded chocolates with an excellent shine.

GORGEOUS GINGER: this was certainly one of the highlights—an excellent light ganache balanced with earthy ginger, and Academy of Chocolate gold award winner 2005.

MELTING MILK: this was a soft mousse truffle, with flecks of milk chocolate on the outside and a very light mousse.

CHERRY IN KIRSCH: the swirled dark and white chocolate dome looks fantastic, and does not disappoint.

RASPBERRY RIOT: this was perhaps overpowered by the freeze-dried raspberry coating, which distracted from the ganache center.

LEMON ZING: made with local lemon curd in a white chocolate ganache, this was a delight that brought back childhood memories.

HOUSE SPECIALTIES: fresh hand-dipped, hand-rolled truffles made with a pure ganache of fresh Dorset cream. Visitors to the shop can watch all the chocolates being made through windows into the factory area.

COUVERTURES USED: El Rey and Callebaut.

CHOCOLAT MODERNE
✳ ✳ ✳

27 West 20th Street, Suite 904 (9th Floor), New York, NY 10011, USA
Tel: (212) 229 4797 Fax: (212) 229 4798
www.chocolatmoderne.com

New York banker Joan Coukos left the world of international banking and Wall Street after a visit to Belgium in 2000. There, she experienced her chocolate epiphany, which came while handling some traditional chocolate molds at the Place du Grand Sablon antiques market in Brussels. Self taught, she opened her Chocolat Moderne business in 2003, leaving behind her desk job to "make the best possible chocolate I can make, according to my exacting standards." A far cry from six years spent in the financial sector of post-communist Moscow!

Her molded creations are in the Belgian style, but generally she uses 61 percent Valrhona dark chocolate. They are not too sweet, and do not contain preservatives or artificial flavourings. A wine expert has been employed to recommend a wine or spirit for some of the chocolates, paired to each particular flavor combination.

In the few years since Chocolat Moderne was founded, Joan's creations have gained a deserved nationwide reputation.

❦ **TASTING NOTES** ❦

The "Mixe Pastorale" assortment was a little large in size, although very attractive—with some chocolates actually sprayed with gold cocoa butter to give a medieval effect.

RASPBERRY RENDEZ-VOUS: this was full of life and zing with its jam filling, while the wild flavor of the Tasmania honey balanced well with its dark and milk ganache.

FILLINGS: some of the soft fondant fillings like the banana flambé worked less well, but the nut croquant fillings seem to be a specialty. A peanut version in the petit bonbons assortment added a typical American touch.

HOUSE SPECIALTIES: "Pursuit of Happiness" petits bonbons with Ukrainian Easter egg designs; and high-quality filled bistro bars—a practical way to enjoy some of the Moderne fillings on the move.

COUVERTURES USED: Valrhona.

THE CHOCOLATE SOCIETY
✵ ✵ ✵ ✵

Clay Pit Lane, Roecliffe, Nr Boroughbridge, North Yorkshire, YO51 9LS, UK
Tel: (44-1423) 322 230 Fax: (44-1423) 322 253
www.chocolate.co.uk

Originally formed in 1991 to further the aims of the "Campaign for Real Chocolate" in the United Kingdom, the Chocolate Society has since been transformed by Alan Porter (one of the founders) into a retail brand, with two shops in London and online sales from their Yorkshire base.

The Chocolate Society's shops are a haven for chocolate lovers, selling their own range of chocolates and Belgravia biscuits. They are also among only a handful of places in the United Kingdom where you can get a decent cup of hot chocolate. Most British hot chocolate seems to be made from weak, oversweet, powdered milk mix—regardless of the quality of the establishment. In contrast, the Chocolate Society use only Valrhona Grand Cru chocolate in theirs.

The company has a close relationship with Valrhona and sells and wholesales many Valrhona products, as well as using Valrhona couverture in their own products.

❦ TASTING NOTES ❦

Many of the chocolates in this collection are actually from the Valrhona range, but these are, of course, of good general quality.

TRUFFLES: handmade from Valrhona couverture, these are without doubt the Chocolate Society's best chocolates. They stand up well against the best you can find, with a medium-hard ganache, and the quality of the chocolate used really shows through in the length.

CHOCOLATE-COATED CANDIED ORANGE: this was also excellent, with a subtle lingering orange.

HOUSE SPECIALTIES: drinking chocolate tins, handmade bonbons from Valrhona, and lifetime membership—for which members receive a hamper of products and access to hidden areas of the website.

COUVERTURES USED: Valrhona.

CHOCOLATERIE BERNARD CALLEBAUT
✷ ✷ ✷

1313-1st Street SE, Calgary, Alberta, T2G 5L1, Canada
Tel: (403) 265 5777 Fax: (403) 265 7738
www.bernardcallebaut.com

Born in Wieze in 1954, Bernard Callebaut is the fourth generation of the famous Belgian chocolate-making family. Following the death of Bernard's father and uncle in the late 1970s, the company suffered a crisis of direction, with many conflicting ideas from various members of the family about what to do with the business. Finally, the company was sold to the Suchard Toblerone group, and the proceeds were divided up between the Callebauts. Today, the company—now merged with French producer Cocoa Barry—processes 15 percent of the world's cocoa bean supply, with annual sales in excess of $3 billion.

After training in Antwerp and traveling extensively, Bernard Callebaut emigrated to Canada in 1983. He set up his own shop in Calgary, going against the advice of many locals who did not believe that such expensive, sophisticated, European chocolates would find a market. Bernard, however, was proved right: after a steady start to the business, its growth has been phenomenal, and Callebaut now has 30 stores in Canada, and four in the United States, as well as distribution in Japan.

❦ TASTING NOTES ❦

The chocolates were molded shells, filled with classic Belgian buttercream centers. A dark chocolate case with a whipped praline, topped with a filbert, was certainly the most interesting. Others tasted similar, but the semi-liquid fondant creams were my least favorite as they were very sweet.

AMARETTO: this was a very soft, smooth buttercream, without any distinct flavor, but with a good smooth dark chocolate shell.

RUM CUP: this had a dark shell, with a double layer inside, and a rich smooth milk chocolate center.

CHESTNUT-SHAPED SHELL: this was filled with a sweet green fondant cream.

HOUSE SPECIALTIES: 47 different centers, with an additional 20 varieties in peak season. Molded Santa Claus and other seasonal shapes.

COUVERTURES USED: Callebaut from Belgium.

CHRISTIAN CONSTANT
★ ★ ★ ★

26 Rue du Bac, 75007 Paris, France
Tel: (33-1) 47 03 30 00
www.christianconstant.com

Having formally trained in the hotel business, Christian Constant was the manager of Maison LeNôtre until 1970. He started his own business on the Rue du Bac in the same year—opening a second shop a few years later in the Rue d'Assas—and became famous for his traiteur (outside catering) service. He was awarded the Coq d'Or for the best traiteur in France in recognition.

As a chocolatier, Constant's reputation is ever increasing, and over the years he has been involved in various projects: research in collaboration with the Institute of Cocoa and Coffee; technical writing on chocolate; and writing a book on chocolate for chocolate lovers. He is currently working on The Great Encyclopedia of Chocolate, and has now opened a restaurant at the Palais de Chaillot, opposite the Eiffel Tower.

Constant, who is a great magician with his chocolate, combines diverse and unusual elements in his ganache centers. His ingredient palate includes exotic teas, flower oils, and spices—Yemeni jasmine and green tea, ylang ylang, neroli (orange blossom), vervain, Tahitian vanilla, vetiver from Réunion, Corinthian rose and grape, cinnamon from Sri Lanka, cardamom from Malabar, Chinese ginger, and saffron stamens.

CHRISTIAN CONSTANT

★ ★ ★ ★

🍫 TASTING NOTES 🍫

From exotic teas to Sicilian mandarin peel, this selection was both diverse and delicious.

NOUGATINE: made from sesame seeds, this was covered in a thick layer of bitter, strong, and fruity chocolate.

PALAIS D'OR: this was very buttery, with a hint of rum.

JASMINE: the subtle green tea and ylang ylang made this very delicate, smooth, and buttery.

VERVAIN: the almost limy flavor was well balanced and smooth.

CHINESE GINGER: this delicious dark, fruity ganache had a good, not-too-overwhelming ginger flavor, and even some lumps.

MANDARIN: this very strong, crystallized mandarin peel from Sicily was coated in dark chocolate, and I was pleasantly surprised by this confection.

GANACHE PRALINE: the pistachio gave this a very fresh, nutty, almost fruity flavor.

HOUSE SPECIALTIES: chocolate orange sticks, ganaches with coffee, and plain ganache. A line of special Easter eggs was created on haute couture themes with the collaboration of Yves St. Laurent, Christian Lacroix, Oliver Lapidus, Andre Courèges, Balmain (Oscar de la Renta), Jean Louis Sherer (Mortensen), and Paco Rabanne.

COUVERTURES USED: various—mainly using Central American cocoa beans from Ecuador, Colombia, Venezuela, Trinidad, Tobago, Grenada, Guatemala, Costa Rica, and beans from Madagascar and Sri Lanka. The varieties used are generally criollo and trinitario.

CHRISTIAN SAUNAL
✯ ✯ ✯

31 Avenue des Minimes, 31200 Toulouse, France
Tel: (33-5) 61 22 53 42 Fax: (33-5) 61 13 29 52

The pâtisserie was started in 1954 by Christian Saunal's father, who before this had worked in all the finest establishments the length and breadth of France. Christian Saunal took over the business in 1974. Although it is primarily a pâtisserie, ice cream parlor, and salon de thé, the chocolate side of the business assumes more importance every year, and Saunal now has a repertoire of more than 50 types of chocolates and 20 different chocolate cakes.

Born in 1946, the young Saunal had a chocolate-immersed childhood, as both of his parents were in the pâtisserie business. He was apprenticed at his father's side, yet also managed to find time to fit in a three-year degree course in physics and chemistry at the Faculty of Science at Toulouse University. Having completed his studies, he dedicated himself to a career as a maître pâtissier and chocolatier, and after a stint in the family business, he went to finish his apprenticeship in the best-known houses in the region.

When he returned to the family business in 1974, his enthusiasm for chocolate had become a real passion. Since then, he has dedicated himself to creating a range of subtle, delicate ganaches that work on two levels: the first notes are floral or aromatic; and the other elements come through more slowly with a really long finish—as one would expect with a fine wine.

❦ TASTING NOTES ❦

The box included some good examples of Saunal's refined "two-level" ganaches.

EARL GREY TEA GANACHE: this was made from Manjari—Valrhona's fruitiest couverture.

DARK ROUND TRUFFLE: this was very smooth with delicate aniseed notes and a long finish.

GUANAJA: this was a very smooth, buttery dark ganache with vanilla.

ARMAGNAC: this was a ganache made from Valrhona Caraïbe and Armagnac.

HOUSE SPECIALTIES: 50 types of chocolate and 20 different chocolate cakes set them apart. Seasonal specialties are marrons glacé.

COUVERTURES USED: Valrhona, Cacao Barry.

CHRISTOPHER NORMAN CHOCOLATES
⋆ ⋆ ⋆

60 New Street, New York, NY 10004, USA
Tel: (212) 402 1243 Fax: (212) 402 1249
www.christophernormanchocolates.com

A painter turned chocolatier, Canadian John Christopher Norman Down graduated in design from the Emily Carr Institute of Art and Design in Vancouver. After moving to New York in the 1980s to pursue his career as an artist, Down met his future chocolate partner, Joe Guiliano. In 1990, they began to make chocolates using John Down's artistic skills to create original, painterly designs and flavor combinations, with packaging to match. The company's reputation grew—with products sold in New York stores such as Balducci's Food Market; and with the attention of celebrity customers such as New York fashion designer Kate Spade, and Martha Stewart.

In 2003, Christopher Norman Chocolates moved from its cramped Lower East Side factory into a new location in Downtown Manhattan. With four times the space, there was now room for a gallery shop—set at the front of the factory. As well as fresh chocolates, customers can enjoy hot drinks and pastries, or peer into the factory area from a street window. John Down continues to paint and exhibits on canvas, as well as on his chocolates.

TASTING NOTES 🍫

The "stained glass" collection was a visual delight. The strawberry balsamic ganache was adventurous, though it may have worked better with a sweeter, less acid balsamic. The Manhattan dark ganache contained a strong vanilla. There were perhaps, however, a few too many fondants in the collection for my personal taste.

GREEN TEA ARBORIO RICE: this was an unexpected highlight—the rice made a particularly light and creamy fondant base for the green tea.

COCONUT CURRY: another delicate fondant, with the curry floating through at the end, though it could have been a little stronger.

WALNUT ROSEMARY: a ganache with a herbal note, but perhaps a little too much butter.

HOUSE SPECIALTIES: an edible cappuccino cup, dark chocolate dominos dotted with white chocolate, and chocolate-coated pears.

COUVERTURES USED: Schokinag.

CÔTE DE FRANCE
✴ ✴ ✴

9 Avenue du Président Salvador-Allende, Vitry-sur-Seine, 94400, France
Tel: (33-1) 46 80 85 06
www.cotedefrance.fr

Côte de France was founded in 1936, and the grandson of the founder continues a tradition of devotion to quality. "Quality... by excellence" has been the philosophy of the company since the outset. It is one of very few Parisian manufacturers that still makes chocolates starting from the cocoa beans— beans that are carefully selected to give the chocolates a long, delicate finish. No artificial preservatives, coloring, nor sweeteners are used, and the products are never deep-frozen. Since 1992, Côte de France has received various prizes at international food and chocolate fairs.

The maître chocolatier is Philippe Wasterlain. Having studied engineering, he learned the art of chocolate manufacture during his school vacations. While continuing his studies, he became an apprentice, eventually joining the family firm that he continues to run today. He is reputed to be one of the few chocolatiers to be able to taste unroasted beans and know what sort of blend they will make.

🍫 TASTING NOTES 🍫

These dark, glossy chocolates displayed good workmanship and contained fine ingredients, but looked rather mass produced, and all had praline centers. The packaging was dull.

SHIP-EMBOSSED MOLDED CHOCOLATE: with dark praline, this was very fresh and crunchy.

VINE LEAVES: the dark chocolate leaf was very good, with a hint of reglisse in the center, while the fatter, milk chocolate version had a smooth praline that was a bit too buttery.

TRAPEZOID-SHAPED DARK CHOCOLATE: this was a crunchy praline with a lingering aftertaste.

OTHER PRALINES: the four-leaf clover of coffee butter and praline, and the dark flower-printed square, were very smooth. Others featured orange zest and crunchy nuts.

HOUSE SPECIALTIES: additive-free produce, noisettines Dinantais, enrobed cookies, and pâté de fruit.

COUVERTURES USED: only its own couverture is used—made from beans whose blend is a company secret. The majority come from South America and Indonesia. The big West African cocoa producers such as Cameroon and Ivory Coast are never used.

DAMIAN ALLSOP CONSULTING
★ ★ ★ ★

Tel: (44-7931) 515 507
www.damianallsop.com

Damian Allsop has a pastry chef's approach, backed by 16 years of experience: first with Robert Mey in New York at the Hyatt Carlton Tower; and then with Gordon Ramsay and Giorgio Locatelli in London. Time spent in Barcelona in the experimental restaurant, Moo, taught Damian to consider food at a molecular level, so it is no surprise that he has been called the "Professor of Chocolate" in the press. Damian has been working on his own unique style of chocolates, and his most recent venture was as the chocolatier behind Melt, in London. He is an honorary member of the Academy of Chocolate, was a judge at the 2005 World Chocolate Awards, and is now busy setting up his own fine chocolate venture.

❦ TASTING NOTES ❦

Damian's chocolates are, unusually, almost all made with water instead of cream or butter. This makes for refreshingly light, wispy textures and a little less guilt about calories. It also means that the delicate flavor and texture of the chocolate he uses can shine through without having to compete with other elements.

MINT DISC: this had fresh mint in a water-based ganache with a very genuine, garden flavor.

PASSION FRUIT AND COFFEE BONBON: this was carefully constructed to release the flavors one by one. The fruity tartness of the passion fruit puree was followed by the coffee surprise as the chocolate melted in the mouth. Best eaten whole then munched for the full effect. Extraordinary!

GINGER MADELEINE: subtle ginger and excellent milk chocolate formed a very rich ganache that you would never know was made from water!

HOUSE ORGANIC DARK TRUFFLE: an exception to the usual water-based technique, this was a very light mousse truffle made with organic cream.

HOUSE SPECIALTIES: water-based ganaches and multi-flavor layered chocolates designed by Damian are sold in Melt, London (page 112).

COUVERTURES USED: Valrhona and Michel Cluizel.

DE BONDT
★ ★ ★ ★ ★

Via Turati 22 (Corte San Domenico) 56125 Pisa, Italy
Tel / Fax: (39-50) 50 18 96

Opened in December 1993 by Dutch pastry chef, Paul de Bondt, and Cecilia Iacobelli—who trained at the Academia de Belle Arti in Carrara, Italy—de Bondt is a relative newcomer to the world of fine chocolate.

De Bondt trained as both chef pâtissier and chef de cuisine, working extensively in four and five-star hotels in the Tuscany region of Italy. His and Cecilia Iacobelli's philosophy is to produce the highest quality chocolates, using only the finest ingredients, the best couvertures, and ganache as a base for the fillings. Carefully chosen ingredients include lemons from Monterosso (Liguria), walnuts from Salerno,

almonds from Sicily, and crystallized orange and lemon peel from organically grown fruit.

The style of the shop and the exquisite packaging—which befits the original and superbly made chocolates—are contemporary as opposed to romantic. Simplicity is the key word here, reflecting Tuscan cuisine: fresh, unpretentious, and most certainly among the world's finest.

Since the first edition of this book was written, I have worked many times with Paul, and he is, without doubt, a truly original character with a hugely generous spirit. He and Cecilia deserve all the acclaim that they receive.

DE BONDT
★ ★ ★ ★ ★

🍫 TASTING NOTES 🍫

Most were very finely balanced and delicate with excellent dark chocolate and a soft consistency. They were beautifully made and finished, and their presentation was superb.

HALF-DIPPED CRYSTALLIZED MELON: this was delicate, beautiful, and not too sweet.

ORANGE GANACHE: diamond-shaped with dark cocoa powder, this was fragrant with a perfectly balanced taste.

LEMON GANACHE: also diamond-shaped with dark cocoa powder, and made with fresh Liguria lemon, this had a fragrant and very natural, good flavor—reminiscent of fresh ginger.

TEA GANACHE: a slightly lighter chocolate than others, this had Earl Grey and perhaps a faint hint of jasmine. Delicious!

GIANDUJA: the delicious and distinctive nut taste was very fresh and slightly grainy.

CHESTNUT HONEY GANACHE: this had a bubblegum taste and a good texture.

HAND-ROLLED TRUFFLE: dusted with cocoa but quite pale, the truffle had a caramel filling. It was smooth and delicate and very good.

WALNUT GIANDUJA: with an interesting, slightly sandy texture, this had a very soft and strong walnut taste—one of the best.

OTHER HIGHLIGHTS: the classic white truffle with a slightly heavier, denser texture than the others; a mendiant of pine nuts, almonds, raisins, and filberts made of dark chocolate; and the rum and raisin ganache with its pleasant soft texture and combination of taste.

COUVERTURES USED: top secret.

DELEANS
★ ★ ★ ★ ★

20 Rue Cérès, Reims, 51100, France
Tel: (33-3) 26 47 56 35

Founded in 1810 by Monsieur Deleans, the business was bought by the current owner and maître chocolatier's grandfather in 1910.

Monsieur J Gaudon, the maître chocolatier, inherited his passion for chocolate over three generations and has been making chocolates since his early childhood, when he learned the tricks of the trade at his father's knee. After studying chocolate making and finally gaining his Brevet de Maîtrise, he became a maître artisan chocolatier. He is a charming example of the old-world artisan chocolatier.

❦ TASTING NOTES ❦

HOUSE SPECIALTIES: Nelusco cherries; Palet Café; almond praline; filbert praline; and pâté d'amande.

COUVERTURES USED: Gaudon makes his own blend using Valrhona and Callebaut, and adding extra cocoa butter and cocoa powder.

DREIMEISTER
★★★

Weststrasse 47-49, D-59457 Werl, Westönnen, Germany
Tel: (49-2922) 8773 0 Fax: (49-2922) 8773 111
www.dreimeister.de

Started in 1953 by the father of the present maître chocolatier, Hans Wilhelm Scröder, Dreimeister was first known as Café Scröder. Its original location was in the shadow of the Basilica in the pilgrim town of Werl, in Germany. The name Dreimeister was adopted in 1973, and the large production unit was opened in 1988 in a converted dairy. In spite of a large turnover, the company prides itself on using only high quality and fresh raw materials—nothing is more than seven days old when it reaches the customer.

❦ TASTING NOTES ❦

HOUSE SPECIALTIES: truffles and seasonal Christmas trees and stars.

COUVERTURES USED: Callebaut and Cacao Barry.

DUDLE
★ ★ ★

Weggisgasse 34, Lucerne CH-6004, Switzerland
Tel: (41-41) 512 767

This is a small family business, started by Karl Habereli-Eizholzer in 1872, and inherited by his son, the young Edourd Dudle, who had first come to work as an apprentice in 1914. Dudle then spread his wings and traveled the world, finally gravitating toward the United States. In 1934, he returned to take over the business; passing it on to his son Max in 1964. Today, Max Dudle's son, Martin, is in charge and, keeping it in the family, has ensured that standards are maintained. No artificial preservatives or flavorings are used.

The maître chocolatier in charge of the 20 employees is Manfred Busch, and everything is still made by hand. Alongside the 1930s style chocolate shop, there is a tea room where customers can relax. Dudle is most famous for its huge milk chocolate medallions, which are available in its shops.

🍫 TASTING NOTES 🍫

HOUSE SPECIALTIES: Dublones—a smooth filbert mousse set in creamy milk chocolate; Luzerne fish—milk chocolate filled with filbert praline; huge gold coins filled with a creamy, honey filling; assorted truffles; and solid chocolate bars with whole nuts.

COUVERTURES USED: Felchlin.

FASSBENDER
✦✦✦

53703 Siegburg, Postfach 13 10, Germany
Tel: (49-2241) 170 70 Fax: (49-2241) 663 22
www.fassbender.de

In 1910, Herr Fassbender opened the first konditorei in Siegburg, Germany, serving coffee, cakes, and chocolates. The business has remained in the family ever since, and in 1989, Herr Fassbender's grandson, maître pâtissier Hans-Werner Fassbender was awarded membership of the famous International Association of Relais Desserts. He is one of only four pastry chefs in Germany today to be so honored. Hans-Werner also won the equivalent of the Nobel prize within the German bakery industry for his entrepreneurial skills in his very specialized trade. He is so dedicated that he often works a 70-hour week: 60 percent of his time is spent in the kitchen; 30 percent in research development; and 10 percent doing administration.

In 1982, Fassbender opened a second shop in Cologne, which inspired some of his Dom (Cathedral)-shaped chocolates and other confectioneries. The company now has a total of five shops around Germany.

FLICKORNA KANOLD
✭ ✭ ✭

Södra Larmgatan 14, 411 16 Göteborg, Sweden
Tel: (46-31) 13 05 61 Fax: (46-31) 93 65 85
www.flickornakanold.com

Scandinavians have a real taste for fine chocolate, and nowhere more than in Sweden. The Swedish chocolate festival, Chokladfestivalen, is backed by the Swedish Chocolate Academy (ChokladAkademien), and is a very popular annual event held at the Nordiska Museet in Stockholm, which receives over 10,000 visitors each year. In recent years, many new chocolatiers have sprung up in Sweden, using good quality couverture and following the example of the fine French chocolatiers.

One such chocolatier is Jeanna Kanold, who founded her own business in 1998. Her family has been in the chocolate business since 1901. Jeanna was educated at The Cordon Bleu Cookery School, London, in 1990, and has always had an interest in creating her own truffles and pralines. She makes all of her chocolates by hand, using chocolate from the French maker Michel Cluizel—who has only recently made a strong push into the couverture market and is still a little underused.

❦ TASTING NOTES ❦

While the ganaches in this selection were well made and not too sweet, I found the fondants tended to lack flavor.

COCOA-DUSTED LEMON TRUFFLE: made with white chocolate, this was tart and creamy.

SALT DARK CHOCOLATE GANACHE: this allowed the Michel Cluizel chocolate to really come through.

LIQUORICE GANACHE: a favorite in Sweden, this was one of the best tasted—subtle and full without being too strong.

HOUSE SPECIALTIES: pralines flavored with spices, malt whiskeys, and fruits.

COUVERTURES USED: Michel Cluizel.

FOUQUET
★ ★ ★

36 Rue Laffitte, 75009 Paris, France
Tel: (33-1) 47 70 85 00
www.fouquet.fr

22 Rue François-1er, 75008 Paris, France
Tel: (33-1) 47 23 30 36
www.fouquet.fr

Since it was founded in 1852, Fouquet has sold a wide range of groceries, including chocolates and other confections that are still made on the premises. The store's location in the bohemian ninth arrondissement of Paris attracted local artists such as Gertrude Stein. In 1926, a second store opened in the fashionable eighth arrondissement on the corner of the Champs-Elysées and Rue François-1er.

Rigorously keeping to traditional production methods and making no compromises by using cheap ingredients, Fouquet uses only the finest quality of raw materials. Currently under the direction of the fourth generation of the family—Mlle Chambeau-Fouquet and her nephew, Christophe—Fouquet imports cocoa beans direct from Venezuela, as well as pure vanilla from Réunion. Using only the freshest ingredients and working on a truly artisan scale, small batches of chocolates are prepared daily. Handmade boxes are packed with two layers of chocolates, and old-fashioned waxed paper and satin ribbon add the finishing touches to the packaging.

FOUQUET

★ ★ ★

❦ TASTING NOTES ❦

This selection of chocolates reminded me of a fine classic English selection from the Empire days—especially by the double enrobing of the chocolates, which is much maligned by the new-wave French chocolatiers, but still boasted of by some English chocolatiers.

DOUBLE ENROBED ORANGETTE: this was not sticky—almost dry, in fact—but quite tangy and not too sweet.

HEART-SHAPED CHOCOLATE: again double enrobed, with toasted almond chunks inside, this was a simple, unpretentious chocolate.

CROUSTILLANT: with its thin, dark chocolate couverture, this had a crispy, croquant, cookie-style center, which was buttery, crunchy, and delicious.

CARAMEL CAFÉ: this coffee caramel in dark chocolate was a bit chewy, but very good.

CARAMEL AU CHOCOLAT: this was a dark gooey chocolate caramel, and a house specialty.

PRALINE DOMINO: this was good, if a little sweet.

STICKY MARZIPAN: this seemed to be doused with liqueur.

HOUSE SPECIALTIES: very hard caramels. Seasonal specialties include: chocolate hearts filled with pralines; molded Easter eggs; fish; bells; and an assortment of chocolates rooted in nineteenth century tradition—sugar-fondant ducks, rabbits, fish, seashells, and flowers.

COUVERTURES USED: top secret.

FRAN'S CHOCOLATES
★ ★ ★ ★

1300 East Pike Street, Seattle, WA 98122, USA
Tel: (206) 322 0233 Fax: (206) 322 0452
www.franschocolates.com

E stablished in 1981, Fran's quickly became known as a serious European-style chocolate maker, whose business was born from a passion for chocolate. Fran Bigelowe had a conventional start to her professional life, graduating and working as an accountant. It was only after her two children were born that she became very interested in cooking and pastry making. She studied with the legendary octogenarian Josephine Araldo in San Francisco, who had graduated from the Cordon Bleu School in Paris in 1921, and had cooked for Georges Clemenceau and Isadora Duncan. After her training with Araldo, Fran Bigelowe enrolled in the newly opened California Culinary Academy in 1976. Throughout the time her children were growing up, she was passionately keen to start her own business. When the day finally arrived and the family moved back to Seattle in 1980, Fran invested her life savings and opened her shop in the Madison Park neighborhood. She says, "It's evolved from one part of the spectrum all the way to another. In the beginning we were

mainly doing desserts for restaurants. Today, it's evolved more and more into a chocolate line of candies and truffles that we've become known for, and we're proud that people are coming back for more." Fran is still very much involved with the chocolate making and more often than not can be found with chocolate-covered hands as she picks up an uncoated chocolate truffle, submerges the morsel in chocolate for a moment, lets the excess ooze through her spread fingers back into the tub, and then puts one perfect piece of candy on a tray.

❦ TASTING NOTES ❦

Since the last edition of this book, Fran's has made a very welcome move from Belgium couverture to French and Swiss varieties, making the chocolates a lot more interesting and distinct.

DARK AND MILK TRUFFLES: these were much improved, and extremely well made. Different finishes had been hand-drizzled on to the chocolates to distinguish the centers, which were carefully flavored without anything too adventurous.

SALT CARAMELS: strictly for the more experimental—with their gray salt coating, these are quite an experience!

HOUSE SPECIALTIES: dark chocolate truffles; Gold bars; hand-dipped fruit and nuts; a range of chocolate and caramel sauces, tortes, brownies, and cheesecakes. Seasonal specialties include ginger, figs, and chocolate coins.

COUVERTURES USED: Valrhona, Scharffen Berger, and Callebaut.

FRANCISCO TORREBLANCA
★ ★ ★ ★ ★

103 Avenida José Martinez Gonzalez, 03600 Elda, Alicante, Spain
Tel / Fax: (34-965) 471 131
www.torreblanca.net

Paco, as Francisco Torreblanca prefers to be known, is one of only four chef pâtissiers in Spain to be awarded membership of the Relais Desserts. Torreblanca makes pastries, chocolates, and jams using ingredients free of colorings and preservatives. Paco's sons, Jacob and David, are now part of the business, and Jacob has followed in his father's footsteps by winning Best Master Pâtissier of Spain in 2003. The company has plans to open flagship stores around the world.

🍫 TASTING NOTES 🍫

Torreblanca's outstanding chocolates have a shelf life of six to eight weeks.

FLAT SQUARE DARK CHOCOLATE PALET: threads of orange and lemon rind were incorporated in a smooth, silky ganache.

SQUARE DARK CHOCOLATE PALET WITH FORK MARKS: the aroma of reglisse—or licorice—was subtly balanced with the rich ganache and the beautifully fine, crisp chocolate on the outside.

MILK CHOCOLATE PALET ARGENT: with a silver leaf on top, this was filled with a fine and delicately perfumed almond and milk chocolate ganache.

COCOA-DUSTED WHISKEY TRUFFLE: bitter chocolate combined well with a rich dark whiskey truffle.

SANDWICH TOPPED WITH MILK CHOCOLATE: with a salty turrón made from pistachio and a sweet milk gianduja, this provided an unexpected combination of sweet and salt—the texture and saltiness were almost reminiscent of porridge.

OVAL MILK CHOCOLATE: this was an unusual blend of butterscotch, caramel, and fragrant Ceylon tea.

POWDERED SUGAR-DUSTED TRUFFLE: this had praline and possibly orange—fine but a bit sweet.

HOUSE SPECIALTIES: very fine chocolates made with saffron, cinnamon, pear, ginger, coffee, tea, filberts, and pistachio; combined with rare chocolate couvertures.

COUVERTURES USED: Valrhona.

GINET
★★★

9 Rue de la Charité, 69002 Lyon, France
Tel: (33-4) 78 42 09 82 Fax: (33-4) 78 37 94 07
www.chocolats-ginet.com

Pierre Ginet, artisan maître chocolatier, who started his company in 1965, prides himself on his rigorous selection of raw materials and their quality, and his company's service to its customers. The company produces "haute couture" chocolates and has won various prizes at French and European chocolate fairs. This prize-winning quality was certainly evident in the beautifully presented, glossy rows of chocolates, and the rich intense chocolate aroma on opening the box.

❦ TASTING NOTES ❦

HOUSE SPECIALTIES: perle noir (black pearl), guignolos de Lyon, foulards de Lyon (Lyonnais scarves), palets d'or, and truffes fleuries.

COUVERTURES USED: Valrhona.

GODIVA
★ ★

Rue de l'Armistice 5, 1081 Brussels, Belgium
Tel: (32-2) 422 17 11 Fax: (32-2) 422 17 00
www.godiva.be

To many people around the world, Godiva represents the finest chocolate money can buy, and it is especially popular in the United States. This huge chocolate empire was founded in 1929 by the Draps family. The business was bought outright in 1966 by Campbell's Soup and is now a huge industrial concern, with 1,400 branches worldwide. The chocolates are made by two factories: one in Belgium, which supplies the European markets; and the other in Pennsylvania, which makes chocolates especially for the U.S. market. The recipes differ according to the market, and the chocolates are always beautifully packaged.

🍫 TASTING NOTES 🍫

The Belgian chocolates I tasted were large, well made, and well presented. Good dark, milk, and white chocolate surrounded very sweet centers. Vegetable fat and both real and artificial vanilla were listed in the ingredients.

DARK CHOCOLATE HEART: this had a very thick shell, with praline inside.

TRUFFLES: a cocoa-dusted truffle may have been double-dipped, with a milk containing vanilla rum, but it was too sweet for me. Another dusted truffle had an outer dark layer and an inner milk layer, and was filled with a smooth, milky truffle.

WHITE FROG CLUSTER WITH NUTTY DUSTING: this had a whipped-up, pale, grainy praline filling with crunchy sugar which, again, I found too sweet. Generally over-rated.

MILK CHOCOLATE CIRCLE: topped with a piped dark chocolate leaf, this had a soft caramel center with a hint of coffee.

HOUSE SPECIALTIES: "All are special—particularly the Belgian Pralines:" Dame Blanche, Autant, Truffle Amere, Cerisette, Coeur de Bruxelles, Milk and Dark, Truffle Fine Champagne, Cascade, Carre Godiva, and Raisin Fine Champagne. Seasonal specialties include chocolate bears, buchettes, and special chestnut and walnut shapes with orange praline.

COUVERTURES USED: milk, white, and dark varieties made from their own patent recipe.

HEDH & ESCALANTE CHOCOLATIER
✳ ✳ ✳

Mariedalsvägen 66, 217 61 Malmö, Sweden
Tel: (46-733) 10 00 53
www.chocolateri.com

Hedh & Escalante was very recently founded by the partnership of Jan Hedh, a famous pâtissier in the Nordic countries, and Maria Escalante, owner of the Chocolatiers Les Trois Roses chain of chocolate shops in Malmö. Jan Hedh and Maria Escalante are two of the most prestigious names in Swedish chocolate.

They set out to make chocolates of the very highest quality, to be sold in Les Trois Roses shops as well as wholesale. Although they mostly use Valrhona couverture, they have recently started producing their own chocolate—made specially for them from "porcelana" type beans grown in Mexico.

❦ TASTING NOTES ❦

These were mostly handmade or rolled truffles and ganaches, with a few molded hearts and shapes. The dark ganaches were of a high standard, but some of the truffles and flavored chocolates seemed a little sweet—in particular, the Baileys dome.

GRAN COUVA GANACHE: making excellent use of a Valrhona vintage chocolate, this had a good length; it was also unusual as this chocolate is normally only available as a bar.

DARK SALT GANACHE: this made an interesting change from the usual salt caramels.

"GIN AND TONIC" GANACHE: this unlikely blend works surprisingly well, though is not as alcoholic as one might expect (or hope!).

SPECIAL PORCELANA GANACHE: this was full of honey butter tones from the chocolate, with a gritty texture and a yeast edge.

HALF GOLF BALL: realistic and rather cute, this contained an excellent smooth, hazelnut praline ganache.

HOUSE SPECIALTIES: pure "neo-porcelana" 100 percent criollo bar, made in the "indian way" from beans from La Joya, Tabasco, Mexico.

COUVERTURES USED: Valrhona, and their own, commissioned Porcelana.

HEINEMANN
★ ★ ★

Krefelder Strasse 645, 41066 Mönchengladbach, Germany
Tel: (49-21) 61 693 0
www.konditorei-heinemann.de

The town of Mönchengladbach, probably most famous for its soccer team, saw the opening of a Konditorei—a coffee house serving pastries and confectionery—in 1932. Established by Hermann Heinemann, the business grew slowly at first, but in 1953 Heinemann took the step of making his own chocolates. They were so successful that, by 1966, he had six shops in four different cities, and it became apparent that a large, modern production unit was needed to supply the growing demand. Heinemann's two sons joined the business as soon as they were old enough, but sadly Bernd Heinemann met an untimely death in 1992. These days, Heinz Richard Heinemann is not only the dynamic chairman of the company—now boasting 11 shops—but also maître chocolatier and member of the International Association of Relais Desserts. Heinz Richard spent 10 years learning the art of chocolate making.

🍫 TASTING NOTES 🍫

CHAMPAGNE TRUFFLE: dusted with powdered sugar, this was exceptional. Inside the milk chocolate shell, there were two halves—a light melting buttercream with lots of alcohol, and a milk chocolate ganache.

PREMOLDED SQUARE CUP: filled with a buttery liquid caramel and topped with an almond croquant, this looked very industrial but had an excellent flavor. Ideal for caramel and milk chocolate lovers.

OTHER TRUFFLES: the milk chocolate truffle with white stripes tasted of a very strong orange alcohol, and lacked subtlety; as did the Cognac truffles.

HOUSE SPECIALTIES: over 60 varieties of chocolate made fresh every day, including orange, cocoa, almond, walnut, kirsch, nougat, and croquant. Seasonal specialties: Santa Claus in many different outfits, Valentine's hearts, Easter eggs, flower bouquets, clowns, animals, and other fun characters filled with chocolates.

COUVERTURES USED: they make their own.

HOVBY NO 9
✳ ✳ ✳ ✳

St. Gråbrödersg. 3, 222 22 Lund, Sweden
Tel / Fax: (46-46) 14 44 88
www.hovbyno9.se

At the age of 50, Inger Persson Clerc was inspired to begin a new career in fine chocolate after reading "La Maison du Chocolat" by the French master, Robert Linxe. After spending time in France, Inger returned to Sweden, opening Chocolaterie Hovby No 9 in the fall of 1998. The shop is named after her family farm, which is in the region where Absolut® vodka has been made since 1879. Inger has created a vodka ganache in celebration of this connection, using Absolut® Mandrin (a new flavor that was launched in 1999).

Inger works in a small-scale factory in an alley next door to the shop, in the central area of the city of Lund in southern Sweden, north of Malmö. Although tucked away, the shop is frequented by both locals and tourists. Inger's motto is to never rush, take great care, and do everything by hand.

❧ TASTING NOTES ❧

The selection included a good range of ganaches in rather large square chocolates.

RASPBERRY: this was thick and jam-like, with a smoky edge and lingering fruit.

LAVENDER: the flavor was a little faint.

CARDAMOM: this was well balanced and not too spicy, with a good length from both the chocolate and the filling.

FENNEL MOUSSE TRUFFLE: this was well made and light, but the flavor might not appeal to everyone. It was also very large, almost like a cake!

COUVERTURES USED: Chocolaterie de l'Opéra, with some Michel Cluizel and Valrhona.

JEAN-PAUL HÉVIN
★ ★ ★ ★ ★

3 Rue Vavin, 75006 Paris, France
Tel: (33-1) 43 54 09 85
www.jphevin.com

Omotesando Hills, 1F 4-12-10 Jingu-
Mae, Shibuya-Ku, Tokyo, Japan
www.jphevin.com

In 1990, Jean-Paul Hévin started a chocolate company in his own name. Voted second best chocolatier in France after Robert Linxe in the 1994 Guide Juillard des Croqueurs de Chocolat, Jean-Paul Hévin is one of the new generation of French chocolatiers. His rigorous training lasted more than 10 years, and he has been winning prizes from the start. In 1986, he won the title Meilleur Ouvrier de France, and first prize for chocolate making in 1988. He has worked under the tutelege of two former winners of this trophy, Joel Rebouchon and Michel Foussart.

Hévin has also worked with Peltier and even opened and ran the Tokyo shop for a year. With this illustrious background, Jean-Paul bought his first shop, a Russian tea-house, Le Petit Boule, in 1988, and created a line of serious dark chocolate delicacies. These days, Hévin is one of the superstars of the chocolate world—especially in Japan. I recently saw his collection of cheese chocolates in Paris, including reblochon and goats cheese. I did not get to taste them as the shop was closed, but such novel combinations certainly challenge chocolate perceptions.

JEAN-PAUL HÉVIN

✴ ✴ ✴ ✴ ✴

❦ TASTING NOTES ❦

Beautifully presented in a caramel-colored box, these were incredibly delicate, and the heady aroma of chocolate made way in due course for fine and subtle fragrances. This is a tribute to Jean-Paul Hévin's exacting methods of tasting, which enable him to detect and balance the multiple levels of flavors hidden deep within each chocolate.

MAUBOURG: this deliciously light praline had tiny pieces of caramelized nougatine.

ESMERALDA: the glossy, fragrant raspberry ganache finely balances the fruit, which emerges slowly on the tongue.

GANACHE AU THÉ FUMÉ: decorated with cocoa spots, the ganache was so light that the smoked tea almost floats away before you capture its fragrance.

ZENZERO: this fruity ginger ganache had a note of deep black licorice that emerged at the end.

KEOPS: this piped succulent pistachio marzipan was covered in the finest layer of intense dark chocolate.

LE PETIT BOULE: the delicate chocolatey caramel melted through the ganache, and neither element overpowered the other.

CAPARUNA: this floral, heather-scented, deep chocolate ganache evoked warm summer days.

LE 1502: this dark, creamy, and buttery ganache was bitter and slightly astringent.

HOUSE SPECIALTIES: seasonal specialties include flat Easter eggs.

COUVERTURES USED: Valrhona.

JOËL DURAND
★ ★ ★ ★

3 Boulevard Victor Hugo, 13210, Saint Remy de Provence, France
Tel / Fax: (33-4) 90 92 38 25
www.chocolat-durand.com

This small shop and salon de thé opened in 1987, and can be found nestling behind a beautiful baroque façade in the historic town of Rennes, in France. From the start, Joël Durand showed his flair and originality in creating special cakes and handmade chocolates. He initially found pâtisserie to be the perfect medium for expressing his ideas, but when he started working with chocolate, his mind went into overdrive—dreaming up all sorts of unlikely flavor combinations and then putting them into practice. Using a ganache as a canvas, Durand experimented with such diverse flavors as lavender, thyme, black pepper, and cloves to create beautifully rounded and delicate epicurean bouchées.

At the age of 28, Joël Durand was the youngest chocolatier to be voted one of the top 10 chocolatiers in France by the Club des Croqueurs de Chocolat. Traditionally every chocolatier has his own "signature"—perhaps a particular shape, or set of molds. For Joël Durand it is a numbering system: each of his 26 chocolates is identified by its own number placed on top of the chocolate palet by means of a cocoa butter transfer. A menu is supplied with each box for decoding purposes. It may be a bit of a gamble when it comes to the six and the nine—they looked the same to me!

Joël has traveled all over the world in search of the perfect cocoa bean, and is now working on creating his own unique couverture.

JOËL DURAND

* * * *

🍫 TASTING NOTES 🍫

Joël Durand specializes in numbered ganaches, with flavors ranging from jasmine tea and thyme to cloves, cardamom, and Chinese pepper.

No.2: this was a milky ganache with a slightly dry texture and lots of orange zest.

No.5: this Earl Grey from "Maison Damann" is a classic, made with a smooth, well-balanced, milky ganache that was extremely fragrant.

No.6: Thé Noël: this was a cinnamon tea from Marriage Frères (Paris Tea Merchant), blended with a smooth and subtle ganache, with a lingering bouquet of cinnamon.

No.7: the jasmine was fragrant and instantly evocative of China, fine and well balanced.

No.9: Menthe Fraiche: this had fresh spearmint leaves infused in a white chocolate ganache—it was delicate, well balanced, and very smooth.

No.10: with lavender, this was a surprisingly good combination of flavors—the lavender takes on a herby flavor, a bit like rosemary.

No.11: nutmeg, cinnamon, lemon zest, and Réunion vanilla made this very festive.

No.12: the best and most original chocolate, this was a perfect marriage of white chocolate and licorice. The initial gentle vanilla notes are followed by melting, bittersweet licorice notes.

No.14: this was a caramel ganache with a strong flavor of burnt sugar; the addition of salty butter adds an interesting twist.

No.16: this was a ganache made with sun-dried Réunion vanilla.

No.24: this black pepper ganache was another unusual but extremely successful combination— it was subtly pungent and the chocolate balanced perfectly with the spice.

HOUSE SPECIALTIES: numbered ganaches, with a variety of unusual flavors.

COUVERTURES USED: Cacao Barry; Durand is also experimenting with making his own couverture, using beans from Guyana and Cameroon.

JOSEPH SCHMIDT CONFECTIONS
✯ ✯ ✯

3489 16th Street, San Francisco, California 94114, USA
Tel: (415) 861 8682 Fax: (415) 861 3923
www.josephschmidtconfections.com

The first shop opened by Joseph Schmidt and Audrey Ryan in 1983 expanded so rapidly that production soon had to move to larger premises, where over 150 personnel—mainly women—are employed. The rationale behind this policy is purely biological: women naturally have cooler hands than men, and all the decorative work on these truffles is done by hand. Temperature fluctuations of just one or two degrees can be critical in chocolate making. Joseph Schmidt's creations look stunning and are probably the most daring that I have ever seen. Audrey Ryan designs and develops the packaging, and also executes the more architectural commissions.

Maître chocolatier Joseph Schmidt was born in 1939 of Austrian parents, but grew up in Palestine. He draws inspiration from his Austrian roots, and that country's tradition of great cakes and chocolates. Trained as a baker, with no formal chocolate apprenticeship, Schmidt eschews the idea of being the pupil of a maître chocolatier: "I don't follow a master's tradition; in Europe everyone learns from a master and follows it like a bible—I like to break tradition. It's just as much fun as keeping it. [Chocolate] is the most fun material in the food business. It gets soft quickly, you play with it, and in a few minutes it's hard as a rock. I would think a lot of creative people would be drawn to chocolate for that reason, but I've been disappointed. The chocolate industry is very, very conservative. Confectioners in Switzerland and France or other places make the same taste, the same shape, year after year." He is so passionate about his metier that he often works 16 and 18-hour days; never turning down commissions, as he believes these to be challenging and inspirational. Schmidt's nocturnal activities sound like something out of a fairy tale: no one, except his partner Audrey Ryan, has ever seen him working on the chocolate creations that appear by day in the shop. After everyone has left the building, Joseph sets to work, mixing his palate of many-colored chocolates, and sculpting masterpieces

which have been compared to Michelangelo, Rodin, and Matisse. His pieces range from exquisite miniatures to gigantic sculptures, including a perfectly scaled-down version of a San Francisco cable car—3 feet high and made entirely from chocolate—which was commissioned for Queen Elizabeth II when she visited San Francisco.

Schmidt does not believe in incorporating nonedible structural supports, and he adores chocolate as a medium because it hardens in minutes, lasts for years, and is also wonderful to eat. He has a nonconformist style and does not use tempering machines—instead opting for a series of plastic buckets, an old pastry oven, and the use of a pilot light. As he says, "I've been pushing my fingers into so much chocolate, it's now in my blood I think." Schmidt does not take himself too seriously, either: "It's really exciting; I love it. When you have fun it shows." And it certainly does.

In 2005, Joseph Schmidt Confections was bought out by the American confectionery giant Hershey, along with chocolate-making neighbor, Scharffen Berger. Indications so far suggest that Hershey will not try to change the quality of either company, but rather help them to develop. Let us hope this continues.

❦ TASTING NOTES ❦

I tasted an assortment of Slicks—thin, glossy disks—which were beautifully crafted and painted with colorful decorations.

ORANGE SLICK: this was white chocolate with a tangy orange butter ganache.

CARAMEL IN MILK CHOCOLATE: the chocolate was very crisp, and the center moist, smooth, and well balanced. The couverture was good with no artificial flavorings.

SCHMIDT'S WHITE CHOCOLATE MUSHROOM: this was really good—not too sweet or cloying— and on the inside was a dark, very smooth truffle with a hint of Amaretto.

HOUSE SPECIALTIES: creations for Valentine's Day, Easter, Mother's Day, Father's Day, Thanksgiving, Christmas, and other seasonal specialties. Special commissions have included a white dove for Nelson Mandela; a giant panda for Prince Philip; a wedding anniversary present for President Reagan commissioned by Nancy Reagan; and the Eiffel Tower for the French Ambassador.

COUVERTURES USED: Callebaut couverture from Belgium.

KNIPSCHILDT CHOCOLATIER
✳ ✳ ✳

12 South Main Street, Norwalk, Connecticut 06854, USA
Tel: (203) 838 3131 Fax: (203) 838 3137
www.knipschildt.com

anish chef Fritz Knipschildt moved to the United States in 1996, having trained in his native Denmark and worked in France and Spain. He worked privately for the "rich and famous," experimenting with spices in his creations. Knipschildt Chocolatier was founded in 1999, producing chocolates entirely by hand with only fresh ingredients, and no additives nor preservatives. Presentation is very important; Knipschildt rejects the idea of standard-sized cut ganaches coated in chocolate, preferring elaborate molds and a range of decorations.

Recently Knipschildt has branched out into a range of confectionery and culinary products, such as syrups, salad dressings, and chocolate cornflake clusters—an interesting quality version of a childhood favorite snack.

🍫 TASTING NOTES 🍫

This was a mostly molded selection made with fairly standard-tasting couverture. Each chocolate had a different girl's name. In general, many of the flavors seemed rather indistinct. A better grade of Valrhona couverture, such as one of the Grand Crus, would really help the whole range.

STACEY: this white chocolate cardamom ganache was well flavored, if sweet.

SOPHIE: this lemon marzipan had only the faintest wisp of lemon flavor.

COUVERTURES USED: Valrhona and Belcolade.

L. HEINER
★ ★ ★

Café Konditorei, 1010 Vienna, Wollzeile 9, Austria
Tel: (43-1) 512 23 43 Fax: (43-1) 512 23 22
www.heiner.co.at

Originally a small baker's shop within the city walls of Vienna, Heiner soon became well known as a café confectioner, becoming official supplier to Kaiser Franz Josephs until 1916.

With each generation, new shops were opened and in 1977 Heiner was awarded the coat of arms of the Republic of Austria. The company is now owned by Paulus Stuller, grandson of Berta Heiner, and his wife Martina, who continue the family tradition.

🍫 TASTING NOTES 🍫

House Specialties: Mozart Kugeln, nougat, truffles, Mandel Orange torte, and Prinz Eugen torte.

Couvertures Used: top secret.

L'ARTISAN DU CHOCOLAT
✦ ✦ ✦ ✦

89, Lower Sloane Street, London SW1W 8DA, UK
Tel: (44-20) 7824 8365 Fax: (44-20) 7730 6139
www.artisanduchocolat.com

At the forefront of the new wave of British chocolatiers, L'artisan was founded in 1999 by Irish pastry chef Gerard Coleman and Belgian business student Anne Weyns. Gerard began his working life as a pastry chef, with stints in New York, before deciding his future lay in producing world-class chocolates in the United Kingdom. After working for the British small industrial producer, Ackermans, Gerard moved on to train with Pierre Marcolini in Belgium. He spent two years with Rococo back in London before branching out on his own.

At first, Gerard produced samples on a very small scale from an industrial estate in Dartford, south of the Thames—working at night in hot weather in a unit with no air conditioning. The first chocolates were aimed at top London restaurants, who Gerard felt would want quality but were not in a position to produce their own fine chocolates. Early samples soon impressed the likes of British celebrity chef, Gordon Ramsay, who asked for an immediate supply. Gerard also set up a stall at one of London's premier "foodie" locations, Borough market, which continues to thrive today.

Soon Gerard was supplying all of Ramsay's restaurants; while the likes of Heston Blumenthal were approaching him to produce a tobacco-flavored ganache for his Fat Duck restaurant. In 2001, the name L'artisan du Chocolat was born, and the shop opened in Lower Sloane Street, near London's Chelsea. At the same time, Gerard's partner, Anne, left her consulting job to join the company full time.

Since then L'artisan's success and reputation have grown in leaps, with an eclectic range of

🍫 TASTING NOTES 🍫

The flavors here were varied and intense.

MOROCCON MINT: this was a pure, light mint ganache, reminiscent of mint in a summer garden, and not too tart.

EARL GREY TEA: a soft, dark ganache, this was flavored with the tea infusion, and had a subtle, bergamot length.

LUMI: beautifully decorated with gold script and red streaks, this ganache was delicately flavored with sun-dried Iranian limes.

PAVE: this was a square, cocoa-dusted truffle with dark and milk ganache layers and crisp,

dark chocolate coating. The chocolate had spice notes and a moreish aftertaste.

LIQUID SALTED CARAMEL: the liquid ganache inside this tiny chocolate shell was too salty for me.

RED WINE: this had a layer of jelly, flavored with Roc Epine, on a dark ganache base.

HOUSE SPECIALTIES: basil, tobacco, and leather ganaches, "O" filled chocolate disks, and their own range of bars—including those using Chocolaterie de l'Opéra chocolate.

COUVERTURES USED: Chocolaterie de l'Opéra, Valrhona, and Michel Cluizel.

flavors individually matched to the flavor notes of a large range of couvertures from several companies. L'artisan's creations can be found in First and Club class on British Airways flights, and were served on the final Concorde flight.

However, their chocolates remain good value. L'artisan generally concentrates on the quality of the chocolates themselves and the flavors; preferring understated, somewhat masculine packaging to more luxurious presentation.

LA BOUTIQUE MICHEL CLUIZEL
✴ ✴ ✴ ✴

201 Rue Saint Honoré, 75001 Paris, France
Tel: (33-1) 42 44 11 66 Fax: (33-1) 42 44 11 70
www.chocolatmichelcluizel.com

This shop is a showcase for Michel Cluizel's chocolate, which is manufactured on a small industrial scale and is widely available throughout France. The company started in 1947 in Damville, Normandy, when retired pastry chef, Marc Cluizel, converted his laundry room into a chocolate production area. The following year, his 14-year-old son, Michel, joined him as his first employee. These days, Michel Cluizel's two daughters and two sons work with him in the business, and have helped Cluizel to become one of the leading lights in the origin chocolate revolution. This is one of the last independent, French, family-run businesses in the chocolate industry that still makes its own chocolate; from the selection of the bean plantation through to the final decorative touches.

La Boutique Michel Cluizel is probably best known for its 99 percent cocoa-bean chocolate bar, which has many devotees (and was recently much improved), and for the five plantation bars—Los Anconès, with beans from Santa Domingo, and Mangaro, with Madagascan beans, being two of the best.

❦ TASTING NOTES ❦

From a milk chocolate ganache with rum-soaked raisins to a sweet fluffy praline in rich bitter chocolate—these chocolates were beautifully presented and very good.

GREEN-FOIL WRAPPED GRAPE: soaked in Marc (white alcohol made from grapes), this had very bitter chocolate.

PALET CACAO DE BRÉSIL: a light marshmallowy ganache, this revealed burnt cocoa at the finish.

PALET CACAO DE JAVA: this was a whipped, buttery truffle, with a rich chocolatey flavor.

PRALINE SAINT-ROCH: undoubtedly the most interesting and successful creation to date, this was a crunchy praline. The unexpected crunch

came from fragments of unrefined, roasted cocoa beans, and the flavor and texture were unique. For those who have never tasted a roasted cocoa bean—an unforgettable experience.

PALET ARGENT: beautifully packaged in a trompe l'oeil bird's-eye maple box, this was a very dramatic and glittery palet with lots of silver leaf. It was filled with a bitter but smooth and buttery ganache.

HOUSE SPECIALTIES: chocolate bars, and autumn boxes filled with seasonal promotions.

COUVERTURES USED: made in-house using beans from Venezuela, Ecuador, Brazil, Columbia, Ghana, Ivory Coast, and Java.

LALONDE
★ ★ ★ ★

242, Avenue Général Leclerc, 54000 Nancy, France
Tel: (33-3) 83 53 31 57 Fax: (33-3) 83 32 51 83
www.lalonde.fr

This house was founded in 1850 by Jean-Frederic Goddefroy Lillig, and from the outset the business was centered on both confectionery and chocolates. With his nephew, Monsieur Lillig invented the Bergamote, which has become a typical specialty of the Alsace region, to the point that Bergamotes de Nancy is now an appellation contrôllée: production is controlled under European law, so Bergamotes de Nancy must be made in Nancy. In 1901, Albert Lalonde took over the business, and the family ran the house until 1970, when it was bought by Fernand Bader. He was joined in 1984 by Jean-Luc Guillevic, who has been running the business since 1994. All the chocolatiers working at Lalonde are trained in-house and customarily stay loyal to their maître until they retire. The recipes, techniques, and trade secrets that have developed over more than 150 years are thus in safe hands, and form an integral part of the business.

Today, in addition to the Bergamotes, the confectionery business is based on Craquelines—nine types of sweetmeat, each with a marzipan base, flavored with a different fruit or alcohol, and encased in a thin layer of caramelized sugar; and the Duchesses de Lorraine, which are almond or filbert pralines encased in royal icing. Quite apart from these sugar confections, Lalonde also makes some of the best artisan chocolates in France.

LALONDE

* * * *

🍫 TASTING NOTES 🍫

Robust 1950s-style packaging had ensured successful transit of the chocolates and preserved the strong fragrance of fine dark chocolate. The chocolates were all hand-dipped, except for one in the shape of a leaf and a dark chocolate palet with a cocoa butter transfer bearing a crown and the Lalonde name.

PALET D'OR: this was faultless—its ganache full of fruit, body, and delicately flavored vanilla, with a smooth melting texture.

GRAND MARNIER GANACHE: this was subtly flavored, dipped in dark chocolate, and perfectly tempered.

RED-FOIL WRAPPED CHERRY: an unusually delicate cherry was preserved in brandy, and housed in a chocolate dome.

HOUSE SPECIALTIES: there are more than 60 varieties of chocolate, which come in three basic types: almond and filbert pralines; ganaches and truffles; and chocolate liqueurs. House specialties include: Pralitas—an almond praline croquante; Pavé du Roi—an almond praline with pistachio; Nelusco—a hazelnut praline flavored with coffee; Stanislas—a pear ganache; and Feuillantines—a grape ganache. Lalonde also do chocolate liqueurs filled with raspberry, mirabelle plum, and kirsch eau de vie; and Chardons de Lorraine, which look like hand-dipped truffles, and are filled with similar liqueurs.

COUVERTURES USED: mainly Valrhona's Caraque and Extra bitter for dark chocolate; and superalpina for milk chocolate.

LA MAISON DU CHOCOLAT
✩ ✩ ✩ ✩ ✩

225 Rue Faubourg St Honoré, Paris 75008, France
Tel: (33-1) 42 27 39 44 Fax: (33-1) 47 64 03 75
www.lamaisonduchocolat.com

Robert Linxe remains the undisputed master of the chocolate world. When he moved to Rue Faubourg St Honoré, Linxe collaborated with fellow Basque artist and designer Arnaud Saez to create the distinctive masculine packaging and the corporate style of La Maison du Chocolat. By the age of 47, despite the risks of starting out on his own, Linxe knew that his individual creative urge was too strong to ignore. He also knew the direction in which he wanted to take French chocolate. Over the past three decades, Linxe has created an image of the finest French chocolate which will surely not be seen as a passing fad, for it is based on an appreciation of the complexities and subtleties of the cocoa bean that a discerning palate can understand. It is in this context that we should look to his collaboration with Valrhona and their production of a line of Grand Cru couvertures that are, in my opinion, the benchmark by which all other fine dark chocolates should be measured. Fine chocolate

will never reach quite the same degree of complexity as fine wine, but Robert Linxe has been instrumental in bringing it to a position where it can be enjoyed by chocoholics and wine buffs alike.

Production has since moved from the wine cellars of the original shop to a purpose-built unit at Colombes on the outskirts of Paris—with 18 employees, including 10 full-time chocolatiers.

Growing up in the Basque region of France, which has a long tradition of chocolate making, must have had an influence, for in 1949 at the age of 18, Linxe decided to change from commercial studies and become an apprentice pâtissier chocolatier. For three years, he worked 14-hour days—a rigorous initiation into the mysteries of a trade filled with secrets and technical know-how. Robert Linxe fueled his passion further by training with the greater master, Jules Perliat, in Basle, Switzerland.

Having completed his studies aged 25, Linxe moved to Paris and worked as a chocolatier

in Neuilly. A year later, with the help of his parents-in-law, he took over ailing chocolaterie, traiteur, and pâtisserie business, La Marquise de Prèsle. After five years, he had established a loyal clientele. This was a time of burgeoning competition, which was emerging after years of austerity; Linxe, however, held his own, gaining widespread recognition. In 1970, Linxe was invited to Japan, where he met Gaston LeNôtre, probably his strongest competition in Paris. LeNôtre proposed a partnership with Linxe, and they began to work together.

Deep down, Linxe could not help but feel that by joining LeNôtre he had let his faithful customers down, so in 1977, when he heard of a wine merchant's for sale in the Rue Faubourg St. Honoré—opposite the famous concert hall Les Salles Pleyelle—he branched out on his own yet again. It was an old shop with large wine cellars, which proved very suitable for chocolate production; and, above all, the location was to provide the inspiration for many of his chocolate creations that have musical counterparts: Bohème, Rigoletto, Faust, Traviata, Otello, Romeo, and Sylvia. The location also ensured a clientele of artists.

La Maison du Chocolat now has stores in New York, London, and Tokyo, and ships its chocolates to many locations worldwide.

🍫 TASTING NOTES 🍫

RIGOLETTO: this was a thin square with a stripe along the diagonal. The milk chocolate couverture contained a caramelized butter—the flavor of the caramel is designed to set off the creaminess of the couverture.

MONT-BLANC: this conical milk chocolate pyramid with a white nipple on top had a ganache made with a whipped butter, and flavored with kirsch. This is an adaptation of a Swiss recipe that Linxe learned in 1952.

LISELOTTE: this was a praline with a milk chocolate couverture; lozenge shaped with lines along the length. The praline is almost a gianduja, with 1/4 filberts to 3/4 almonds.

GUAYAQUIL: this was a large flat square with a slightly wavy surface. It had a dark couverture, with semibitter ganache made with Ecuadorian beans. There were some vanilla notes and it was very light.

QUITO: this was a bright, shining palet with a very fine dark chocolate coating. The ganache had a very powerful aroma and very long finish due to the mix of Venezuelan, Ecuadorian, Trinidadian, and Madagascan beans.

ANDALOUSIE: filling a rectangle with dark couverture, the ganache was made from three types of criollo beans—Venezuelan, Caribbean, and Ecuadorian. This was delicately flavored with lemon; a more difficult pair to combine than chocolate and orange.

ROMEO: this was a dark chocolate couverture rectangle with stripes across the width, and the ganache was a butter mocha—the coffee flavor coming from freshly filtered coffee.

HOUSE SPECIALTIES: chocolates with musical counterparts.

COUVERTURES USED: Valrhona.

LA PRALINE CHOCOLATIER
★★★

2a Avenida de los Palos Grandes, Edificio Artelito, Local 4, Aptdo 2389,
Carmelitas, Caracas, Venezuela
Tel: (58-2) 2 84 79 86 Fax: (58-2) 2 85 2 75

The company was founded in 1985 by Belgian ex-patriots Ludo and Lisette Gillis, who finally settled in Venezuela after sojourns in Brazil and Argentina. Coming from a country with a tradition of producing handmade chocolates in every small village, Ludo Gillis was bowled over by the quality of Venezuelan cocoa. He felt that the best place to learn how to make chocolates was his homeland, Belgium, so he spent a year in Antwerp, training with maître chocolatier Hans Burie. This placement was hard won, and in a small country like Belgium where professional secrets are jealously guarded and normally kept strictly within the family, Ludo had to swear that he was not going to open up around the corner in competition. Gillis also took classes at the Piva school, with famous professors such as F Adriaenssens and Roger Geerts.

Now thoroughly grounded in the skills of chocolate making, Ludo and Lisette Gillis returned to Caracas to set up their own air-conditioned production unit. As Venezuela is located in the tropical zone, even winter daytime temperatures often average 70°F (21°C), which means that the locals have no

LA PRALINE CHOCOLATIER
★ ★ ★

preconceived ideas about chocolate seasons: they just love to eat it all year round! With locally grown fine criollo beans, which are so hard to come by in Europe, and fresh macadamia, cashew, and brazil nuts, a unique collection of tropical chocolates has evolved.

The Venezuelan couverture manufacturer El Rey has collaborated with the Gillises to produce a premium-quality chocolate, using the rarest cocoa beans available and conching the chocolate for much longer than they had been accustomed to.

🍫 TASTING NOTES 🍫

This was a classic Belgian assortment of well-crafted molded chocolates. As fresh cream is used, they must be eaten very quickly.

MAIZE CHOCOLATE MOUSSE: this was very fluffy with a sweet filling.

HEART: this was a Cointreau ganache in dark chocolate.

MACADAMIA MARZIPAN: this was definitely the most interesting and successful chocolate, incorporating chunks of macadamia.

CUPID: this was a very buttery caramel with a slightly burnt taste.

TREE TRUNK: this was a good, slightly crunchy croquant.

CARIBE-MOKA: not too sweet, this was very good.

MARZIPAN: this had a good grainy texture of fresh ground nuts, but was too sweet.

HOUSE SPECIALTIES: macadamia marzipan and cashew praline.

COUVERTURES USED: El Rey couverture made with rare Venezuelan cocoa beans in dark and milk chocolate, with a particularly fine and mild aroma. White couverture is imported from Belcolade in Belgium.

LAURENT GERBAUD
✹ ✹ ✹

Centre Dansaert, Rue d'Alost 7, 1000 Brussels, Belgium
Tel: (32-2) 213 37 20 Fax: (32-2) 213 37 26
www.chocolatsgerbaud.be

Belgian chocolates are often seen as being among the best in the world, but this is partly due to the successful marketing campaigns of the big name brands. Often, chocolates bearing the name "Belgian," both inside and outside of Belgium, are simply far too sweet. Brussels does have a fine chocolate tradition though; a tradition in which Brussels native Laurent Gerbaud grew up. His Belgian tastes were radically changed—from sweet to strong and savory—after time spent in China. There, he made chocolates with local ingredients, experimenting with new tastes and flavor combinations. Laurent is allergic to fresh fruit (although not dried fruit), and

this has influenced his unusual selection of ingredients. On returning to Belgium, Laurent started producing chocolate wherever possible, recruiting members of his family to help. Soon he was producing a range of coated fruits— such as kumquats from Shanghai and exotic chocolate bars sprinkled with salted nuts and dried fruit—using imported ingredients from around the world, including China.

Laurent began his quest using Callebaut chocolate, but after a few years of production he discovered Domori, a new Italian chocolate maker. Domori makes chocolate from the bean in what they call a "low impact" style, where they try to process the beans as little as possible

LAURENT GERBAUD
* * *

🍫 TASTING NOTES 🍫

CHOCOLATE BARS WITH NUTS: the 50 percent salted milk chocolate bar with salted, roasted pistachios was certainly very different—it might not appeal to everyone, but can be very moreish. The salted cashews on dark chocolate had a more subtle flavor, with the cheesy texture of the cashews combining well with the chocolate.

FRUIT CHOCOLATES: dried, Persian cranberries worked very well with the citrus Madagascan notes in the chocolate; while the chocolate-coated Shanghai kumquats were a triumph.

HOUSE SPECIALTIES: l'Invitation au Voyage—a series of nine flavored mini-bars; and an advent calendar made with individual chocolate coins containing nuts and fruit.

COUVERTURES USED: Domori.

in order to produce their finished chocolate. Apparently, this preserves the authentic flavor of the cocoa beans and has the least effect on the flavinoids present in cacao, which have potential health benefits. This gives the chocolate a creamy, or waxy texture—depending on whether or not you like it. Laurent uses a blend made for him with beans from Madagascar and Ecuador, which has fruity, sour notes that combine well with the exotic ingredients he uses.

LE ROUX
✯ ✯ ✯ ✯

18 Rue du Port-Maria, F-56170 Quiberon, France
Tel: (33-2) 97 50 06 83 Fax: (33-2) 97 30 57 94
www.chocolatleroux.com

Le Roux Caramelier-Chocolatier was founded in 1977 by Henri Le Roux and his wife Lorraine in the spa and seaside resort of Quiberon. Originally, the shop sold ice cream and chocolate, but the popularity of the chocolates soon took over, making the ice cream redundant. Le Roux has achieved national and international success, partly due to the creation of the famous, and much-imitated, Caramel au Beurre Salé (salted butter caramel). The chocolates are exquisitely made in the best of French traditions—very rich in chocolate and butter, not too sweet, and extremely delicate—while their technical virtuosity may owe much to the Swiss chocolate-making tradition.

Henri Le Roux, the maître chocolatier, is the son of a pâtissier who worked in the United States, Australia, and France, where Henri was exposed to the world of pastry and chocolate from an early age. After a rigorous

LE ROUX

* * * *

apprenticeship in the Swiss tradition, Le Roux returned to his place of birth, Pont l'Abbé, where he rounded off his education, carrying on the secrets that his father had left behind. He has proved to be one of the great innovators with his Caramel au Beurre Salé, his Petites Douceurs Gourmandes ("little sweetmeats"), and other original recipes. Now very big in Japan, Le Roux has embarked on a joint venture with the hugely successful chocolate biscuit company, Yoku Moku.

🍫 TASTING NOTES 🍫

This was a good selection of original recipes that are inspired by the French tradition.

CORTÉS: aromatic and melting, this was a rich chocolatey ganache on a base of almond praline.

CBS: this chewy caramel with a salty tang, which comes from the salted butter, was an outstandingly successful combination of sweet and salt, with the addition of crunchy almonds and hazelnuts.

KYRA: a very delicate coffee ganache, Kyra had a slightly grainy texture, and a little Cognac.

SUZETTE: this crunchy walnut praline was rather sweet.

SYLVIE: the plain ganache was smoothly bitter—and was a melting combination.

TANTZOR: this was a ganache made from pure criollo beans, and seated on a layer of ginger marzipan.

LOUISON: a caramel made with fruit, this was enrobed in the finest layer of chocolate.

HAREM: a ganache made with mint tea, this was apparently inspired by the freshness of an oasis.

HOUSE SPECIALTIES: Henri Le Roux and truffle king Jacques Pebeyre collaborated in 1989 to create a smooth dark chocolate truffle, with small pieces of fresh black Périgord truffle, which won two Coq d'Or awards. I did not have an opportunity to taste this creation, but am told that it is an exquisite combination, with the delicate perfume of the truffle coming through. It is available during the truffle season: October to February.

COUVERTURES USED: French-made.

LETUFFE
★ ★ ★

10 Place Francis Louvel, 16000 Angoulême, France
Tel: (33-5) 45 91 05 21 Fax: (33-5) 45 91 24 92

The chocolate business that had been founded in 1873 in Angoulême, in the Charente Maritime region of France, was bought by the Letuffe family in 1950. They produced traditional artisan chocolates; introducing new technology by way of an enrobing machine in 1955. When the current director, Jean-Pierre Letuffe, took over the business, he focused production on regional traditions, drawing inspiration from their own local ingredients—beurre de Charentes and crème fraîche are used in the chocolate recipes.

🍫 TASTING NOTES 🍫

When opened, the box—beautifully wrapped and presented in crisp, white pleated paper—revealed a rather incongruous, modern, glossy black and red ballotin inside, and the smell of orange that pervaded the whole box was a little overwhelming. The creamy, buttery, Charentais tradition came through very strongly, but the chocolate itself tasted rather bland, with vanilla and orange flavors predominating.

MILK CHOCOLATE TULIP: this was very sweet.

VIOLET PETAL CHOCOLATE: made with vanilla and almond essence, this contained a ganache flavored with licorice.

ALCOHOLIC CHOCOLATES: generally, the alcohol was overpowering. Chocolat au Pineau de Charentes, a dark chocolate shell with a sugar crust, had very strong alcohol inside; and there were several chocolates that were filled with a fiery eau de vie—possibly Pineau de Charentes—which was almost too strong.

NUTTY CHOCOLATES: these were a bit soggy, making it difficult to identify whether they were almond or pistachio.

HOUSE SPECIALTIES: Palets d'Or; Salamandres—a chocolate cream flavored with raisins and milk caramel, and derived from the coat of arms of François 1; Cognaçais—a chocolate depicting the coat of arms of the town of Cognac; and Marguerite d'Angoulême—which was created as a tribute to Marguerite de Valois, sister of François 1. Other chocolates are made with the local cream, butter, and alcohol.

COUVERTURES USED: top secret.

LINDT & SPRÜNGLI
✳

Seestrasse 204, CH-8802 Kilchberg, Switzerland
Tel: (41-1) 716 22 33 Fax: (41-1) 715 39 85
www.lindt.com

L indt is one of the oldest Swiss chocolate companies, and its founder Rudolphe Lindt (1855–1909) was to revolutionize the manufacture of chocolate with his invention: the conching machine. With this, the particles of chocolate could be ground so finely that, with the addition of cocoa butter, the first melt-in-the-mouth chocolate bar was born. Lindt and Sprüngli came into existence when another great Zurich chocolate family, the Sprünglis, took over the factory. Johann Rudolphe Sprüngli bought the trademark and rights for the vast sum of 1.5 million gold francs. The company produces a huge variety of chocolate bars, assortments, eggs, and couvertures. While Lindt's current range of products are a cut above high street confectionery, they can still only be described as industrial—although the unflavored dark Excellence bars are passable.

🍫 TASTING NOTES 🍫

HOUSE SPECIALTIES: Grand Cru bars, Lindor cornets, Lindt Orange thins, and Easter eggs.

COUVERTURES USED: their own, made to their own unique and original recipe using bean varieties from Trinidad, Grenada, and Ghana.

MARY
★ ★ ★

73 Rue Royal, 1000 Brussels, Belgium
Tel / Fax: (32-2) 217 45 00
www.marychoc.com

Marie Delluc founded the chocolaterie-confiseur, Mary, in 1919. She was appointed the first chocolate supplier to the Belgian royal household in 1942; a warrant that has since been renewed in 1990 and 1994. The business has remained in the family's hands into a third generation, where the maître chocolatier is Jean Lamberty—who fulfilled his childhood dream of becoming a chocolate maker when he married into the family. In 1998, the chocolaterie was taken over by Mr and Mme Boey, who maintain the old traditions.

These chocolates are molded into simple shapes, quite large and well crafted, and have very rich, creamy, and buttery fillings. They are wrapped in gold foil, which is unusual for fine chocolates as it hides their gloss and the skill that went into their creation. The buttery ganache is not overly sweet, as is so often the case with Belgian chocolates.

❦ TASTING NOTES ❦

CHOCOLATE CUPS: the cup with an almond brittle lid contained praline dotted with croquant, but was too sweet. Another dark cup with a milk lid housed a very runny brandy buttercream, colored with chocolate.

MILK CHOCOLATE BASKET: finely chopped almonds added texture to a rich and sweet coffee buttercream center.

DARK ICE CUBE SHAPE: the buttercream filling resembled cake icing, with black specks of Bourbon vanilla. Sadly, it was too sweet.

HOUSE SPECIALTIES: the line consists of 72 different varieties—all handmade and no artificial coloring or flavorings are used.

COUVERTURES USED: made by Callebaut from a choice of 440 blended beans couvertures.

MAZET DE MONTARGIS
✱ ✱ ✱

Place Mirabeau, Montargis, France
Tel: (33-2) 38 98 63 55
www.mazetconfiseur.com

Legend has it that the praline was the result of an accident in a kitchen in 1671. The Duke of Plessis-Praslin, known for his love of good food, was waiting impatiently for his dessert, and unfortunately—or perhaps fortunately—the clumsy kitchen boy had dropped a bowlful of almonds on to the floor. The enraged chef went to box his ears and managed to compound the problem by spilling a pan of hot, burnt sugar over the almonds. The Duke smelled a delicious aroma wafting into the dining room and demanded to taste this new confection. He was so delighted that he modestly coined them "Praslin."

The cook, Clément Lassagne, eventually left the Duke's service to found a confectioner's shop in Montargis, 68 miles south of Paris. Since then, "Praslin" has undergone many changes, but the delicacy can still be recognized in its earliest form, as made by Mazet de Montargis from the original secret recipe. Other variations known as "praline"

can be found in evidence throughout the chocolate world; often used simply to describe chocolates that contain nuts. In the United States, "praline" refers to a round, flat confection, made of pecans embedded in butter, cream, and brown sugar. Pecans are used because almonds and hazelnuts are not readily available.

The Confiserie du Roy, in existence in Montargis since 1647 and famous for its "praslines," was bought in 1902, and its name changed to Mazet de Montargis. The third generation of the Mazet family still owns and runs the beautiful historic shop in Montargis, as well as one in Paris.

❦ TASTING NOTES ❦

The house specialties include a selection of truffles and chocolates, and they also have fruit paste, almond paste, and marron glacés.

AMANDAS: these were almond nougatine dipped in chocolate and cocoa.

MIRABOS: these had a filbert and orange nougat covered with milk chocolate and cocoa.

OTHER NUTTY SPECIALTIES: these included Passions—chocolate-covered sugared almonds; Lyette—chocolate-covered sugared filberts; Grelons—sugared filberts covered in milk chocolate and sugar; and Givrettes—sugared almonds covered in milk chocolate.

PRASLINES: caramelized, grilled almonds.

HOUSE SPECIALTIES: those already described; and seasonal specialties, such as hand-blown real hen's eggs stuffed with chocolate praline, and perfect imitations of quail's eggs—they call them "seagull eggs"—that are praline with sugar speckled shells, for Easter. They also make novelties for Valentine's Day.

COUVERTURES USED: Chocolate du Pecq (78230 Le Pecq), Americao with 72 percent of cocoa using beans from South America and Africa, and Milk Extra with 37 percent of cocoa using beans from Africa and Indonesia.

MELCHIOR CHOCOLATES
★ ★ ★

Tinto House, Station Road, South Molton, Devon EX36 3LL, UK
Tel: (44-1769) 574 442
www.melchiorchocolates.co.uk

In 1977, Swiss-born Carlo Melchior opened a seaside restaurant in the West Country with his English wife. Unable to find any really good-quality chocolates to serve with after-dinner coffee, Carlo, with a strong vision and conviction about chocolate, decided to try his own hand. Remembering what Swiss chocolates tasted like, Melchior quickly realized that he was capable of producing something very similar himself. Encouraged by the glowing feedback of his restaurant clientele, Melchior took the radical step of selling the restaurant, and relocating to the small Devonshire village of Chittlehampton. There, they bought a property with outbuildings and soon converted them into a kitchen and chocolate workshop. Carlo's first client was Fortnum & Mason in London. The store is now one of Melchior's best customers, and has even developed a line of specialty chocolates with them. Since then Melchior has expanded its market to include a number of specialist outlets throughout Britain.

❦ TASTING NOTES ❦

These are beautiful, skillfully made, classic Swiss-style chocolates. Some combinations, such as strawberry and banana with white chocolate, might not find favor with French purists, but no doubt have their aficionados.

DARK TRUFFLES: these were rich, smooth, and alcoholic, with excellent milk champagne, kirsch, and framboise.

RECENT ADDITIONS: these include smooth, buttery truffles made from Valrhona Grand Cru Guanaja and Caraïbe chocolate, and liqueur chocolates made from basic couverture.

HOUSE SPECIALTIES: fruit and liqueur truffles; liquid center liqueur chocolates; personalized chocolate logos; and Christmas novelties.

COUVERTURES USED: Max Felchlin, Maestrani.

MELT
✼ ✼ ✼ ✼

59 Ledbury Road, Notting Hill, London, W11 2AA, UK
Tel: (44-20) 7727 5030
www.meltchocolates.com

Newly opened in 2006, the stylish Melt shop is in the heart of fashionable Notting Hill in west London. Somewhere between a chic boutique and trendy bar, Melt offers a new kind of chocolate shop experience. Founded by local mum and business woman Louise Nason and British pastry chef Damian Allsop (an honorary member of the Academy of Chocolate), Melt aims to bring a more accessible approach to fine chocolates.

Walk into the shop and you will not find carefully protected bonbons in glass cabinets and an offhand attitude. Instead, collect a wooden tray and help yourself to the fresh creations lined up on marble shelves along the wall. Or you can take a few steps further down into the kitchen area, sit on a bar stool, and watch the fresh Melt creations in production, just over the counter.

All of Melt's chocolates are made on site. They contain no preservatives and little sugar,

and organic raw ingredients are used wherever possible. Many of the ganaches use water rather than cream which, although unusual, results in a clean, delicate taste. The chocolates are also beautifully packaged, and bespoke confections can be ordered for special occasions.

MICHAEL RECCHIUTI
✷ ✷ ✷ ✷

One Ferry Building, Shop #30, San Francisco, CA 94111, USA
Tel: (415) 834 9494
www.recchiuti.com

Michael Recchiuti began his chocolate life as a boy, baking Italian wedding cakes alongside his grandmother in Philadelphia. As a young man, he created plated desserts at renowned local restaurant, Le Bec Fin, and later trained with Alain Tricou (Maxim's, Le Cirque) for three years in sugar and chocolate. This awoke a passion for chocolate and innovative flavor combinations, and soon he was traveling west in search of fresh and exotic ingredients. He arrived in San Francisco in 1987. After 10 years of experimentation, where he developed some of his now famous flavors—Tarragon Grapefruit, Lemon Verbena, and Star Anise and Pink Peppercorn—Michael finally launched Recchiuti Confections with Jacky, his wife. His philosophy was that "once you introduce truly exquisite chocolates to people, they will be won over instantly and forever." To this end, he visited San Francisco's farmers' market for bundles of fresh lavender, tarragon, and lemon verbena for his signature infusions, and spent time with the emerging local chocolate makers, choosing the right chocolate for his blends.

To begin with, Michael sold his chocolates from an ice chest at the farmers' market where

he found many of his ingredients. When the new Ferry Building Marketplace opened in 2003 near the Embarcadero district of San Francisco, Michael jumped at the chance to open his store in the renovated historic building. There, he now sells his artistically decorated creations: the chocolates feature drawings, etchings, and paintings from his favorite San Francisco artists, or Japanese block prints, inspired by his Hawaiian wife.

🍫 TASTING NOTES 🍫

This was an extensive range of interesting flavors and varietal dark chocolate ganaches.

STAR ANISE AND PINK PEPPERCORN: not all of the flavors hit the mark, but this—with a semisweet ganache coated in milk chocolate—was very stimulating.

LEMON VERBENA: this was well blended with cream, and hangs very well on the tongue without being too herbal.

CARAMEL: the rose geranium oil used created an excellent, light caramel.

VARIETALS: the Columbian was smooth and buttery, while the Ecuador was robust.

KEY LIME FLORIDA APPLES: these very thin slices of dried, large apples had a wonderful crunch under their fine coating of dark chocolate.

HOUSE SPECIALTIES: Burnt Caramel—a dark chocolate ganache blended with dark, smoky caramel; and the Fleur de Sel Caramel—smoky, burnt caramel flecked with French sea salt.

COUVERTURES USED: El Rey, Valrhona, E Guittard, and Scharffenberger.

MICHEL CHAUDUN
★ ★ ★ ★ ★

149 Rue de l'Université, 75007 Paris, France
Tel: (33-1) 47 53 74 40
www.michel-chaudun.jp

Having opened his own shop in 1986, itself a masterpiece of order and harmony, Michel Chaudun is often to be seen behind the counter, welcoming locals and celebrities with equal warmth. When he is hard at work in the laboratory behind the shop, his wife takes charge in the shop.

Chaudun started his apprenticeship some 30 years ago, at the age of 14. He trained as a chocolatier, glacier, and pâtissier before arriving in Paris, where he worked in all the best chocolate houses: notably Robert Linxe's La Maison du Chocolat, and Maison LeNôtre. He also traveled abroad, working with Swiss chocolatier Withmer. He specializes not only in making some of the finest chocolates in the world, but also in creating the most unbelievable sculptures in chocolate. Winning a prize for his replica of Tutankhamen in 1965, Chaudun has been winning international prizes and receiving accolades from his fellow professionals ever since. Some of the more unusual commissions include gasping puffer fish, halfway to becoming sashimi (presumably commissioned by a Japanese client), and a pair of false teeth that would look perfectly at home on a Halloween candy counter.

Michel Chaudun remains faithful to his philosophy of "giving oneself pleasure and giving pleasure." As he says, "Good chocolate is that which wakes people up with a 'choc'."

🍫 TASTING NOTES 🍫

From the whole range of 30 or so different chocolates—including subtly flavored ganaches and pralines, all hand-enrobed rather than dipped—each chocolate was perfection and became my benchmark of really fine quality. None of the chocolates were molded.

COUVERTURE SQUARES: these had an exquisite bouquet and finish, and were presented in a beautiful box that opened like a cigarette box.

PALET D'OR: this was a very smooth ganache of rich chocolate flavor with a long finish.

VERAGUA: this praline caramel was very good, though rather sweet.

DARK CHOCOLATE DISKS: these had tiny fragments of crunchy roasted cocoa nib crushed into them, with a smooth couverture that was intense and that melted easily.

DOME-SHAPED DARK CHOCOLATE: tipped with white chocolate, this was a succulent rum-soaked raisin on a bed of almond paste, with a dark ganache on top. It was very good.

ORANGETTE: this was really delicious—among the best I have ever tasted. The orange rind had no pith and was very fine in texture, and the dark chocolate surrounding it was studded with toasted almonds. A sensational combination.

COUVERTURES USED: the best French couvertures, made from rare South American criollo and trinitario, Venezuelan, and arriba beans from Ecuador. African and Ivory Coast forastero beans are used to give robustness and balance to the other fine beans.

MICHELI
★★★

1 Rue Micheli-du-Crest, 1205 Geneva, Switzerland
Tel: (41-22) 329 90 06 Fax: (41-22) 781 40 34

Husband and wife team Pierre and Liliane Poncioni have devoted the last 30 years of their lives to this chocolate business. Pierre makes the chocolates, while Liliane runs the shop, and in spite of their long hours, both remain smiling—they just love their work. Their daughter Jannick and their son Didier are also involved in the business: Jannick makes the cakes for the little tea room, where in the summer you can also eat ice cream on the terrace, and Didier does all the paperwork.

Micheli should win a prize for being the only Swiss chocolatier to specialize in dark chocolate; not any old dark, but pure, unadulterated, 100 percent cocoa bars. Explaining his passion for dark chocolate, Pierre says, "To begin with everyone loves milk chocolate, then you change. It's like wine: Burgundy is what all the great wine lovers end up with."

MICHELI

✶ ✶ ✶

❦ TASTING NOTES ❦

DARK CHOCOLATE WITH AN ALMOND: filled with a subtle and delicately crunchy praline, this had a hint of orange.

TRIANGULAR SHAPE IN DARK CHOCOLATE: this was filled with caramelized almonds and a milky praline, with a lingering nutty flavor. It was very good, although a little difficult to eat, because it tended to fracture as it was bitten into.

NOISETTE SANDWICH: with orange on the outer layers, this was very sweet, slightly artificial-tasting, and gritty in texture; also, the orange flavor had tainted its neighbors in the box.

PIPED MILK CHOCOLATE: this looked enticing, but concealed a glacé cherry—not my favorite combination. One to be reserved for the very sweet toothed!

ROUND DARK CHOCOLATE BALL: filled with a very strongly alcoholic truffle and marzipan, the chocolate shell was beautifully crunchy, the ganache very smooth, and the marzipan quite grainy. An interesting combination of textures and flavors, dominated by the alcohol.

RECTANGULAR DARK CHOCOLATE: the crisp shell gave way to a sweet praline, full of freshly toasted nuts, well balanced by the very bitter chocolate on the outside, and with a good long finish.

100 PERCENT BRAZILIAN COCOA BAR: this did not have a very distinctive aroma and was slow to melt in the mouth. It was an interesting experience, though, and perfect with a cup of really bitter espresso coffee.

HOUSE SPECIALTIES: 75, 85, and even 100 percent cocoa chocolate bars; truffles; Pavé Genevois; ice cream; cakes and tea.

COUVERTURES USED: top secret.

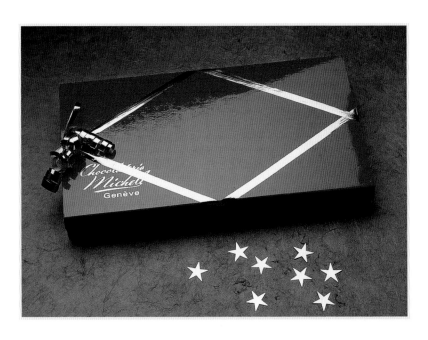

MOONSTRUCK CHOCOLATIER
✷ ✷ ✷

6663 SW Beaverton-Hillsdale Highway, Suite 194, Portland, Oregon 97225, USA
Tel: (503) 283 8843 Fax: (503) 283 8913
www.moonstruckchocolate.com

This very slick marketing company has an impressive panel of experts: Dean Stearman, former marketing director of Godiva USA (also former vice president of Barton Chocolates); Dr Schouten, professor of marketing at the University of Portland, who is also a behavioral market research analyst for companies, including Harley-Davidson—"the ultimate mean motorbike;" and finally William Simmons, the founder of the company, who has extensive experience in the food industry. Simmons had concluded in earlier research that "there is a direct link between the changes that started... in the coffee industry [in the United States] of the 1980s, relative to fine beans, and an opportunity of similar proportions awakening in the chocolate industry in the 1990s." These gentlemen have plans to take the U.S. chocolate market by storm. The packaging is fun and beautifully produced. The chocolates are made with great care and ingenuity, and the "book" box, certain to become a collector's item, states the company's aims and objectives in fairy-tale language in the opening pages: "Much like Merlin, who aged backward in King Arthur's Camelot, and thus knew what the future held, Moonstruck Chocolatier started out with the common chocolate of today. They then researched backward, looking for the non-sweet purity of the chocolate of the past.

❧ TASTING NOTES ❧

The samples I tasted were very well made; the fillings well balanced and sensual with a traditional sense of fun. I must confess that although the chocolate itself was smooth and melting, without any unpleasant "notes," the fillings and the use of a fair amount of milk chocolate meant that it was hard to distinguish any rare flavor beans in the chocolate.

MILK CHOCOLATE HEART: filled with pecan gianduja and soft caramel, this was very good—delicate, and not too sweet.

WILD HUCKLEBERRY TRUFFLE: a jam-like filling and a white chocolate ganache resulted in a very sweet chocolate.

GIANDUJA ALMOND PRALINE TOWER: this had a very good, crisp butter toffee and roasted almonds.

CLEAR CREEK APPLE BRANDY TRUFFLE: this was a very subtle caramelly truffle.

PURE GOLD TRUFFLE: this rather large bittersweet ganache, the filling darker than the covering, and with honey and Drambuie, looked very dramatic, especially with the gold leaf embellishment.

ESPRESSO ITALIA TRUFFLE: this tasted like a cup of capuccino, with good flavor and a silky texture.

TOFFEE TRUFFLE: this was actually a rather light ganache, coated with white chocolate and elegantly decorated. It had a subtle flavor of butter toffee without being overly sweet.

OCUMARIAN LOGO TRUFFLE: the one truffle of the collection labeled as being made with a varietal chocolate, this had an added healthy spike of chili. The dark earth notes of the chocolate suggest a couverture in the Spanish style.

HOUSE SPECIALTIES: moon-shaped boxes, a selection of truffles, and chocolates including wine, brandy, saké, fruit, and coffee.

COUVERTURES USED: Moonstruck sources chocolate liquors and makes its own couverture, adding 38 to 40 percent cocoa butter and selecting fine and flavorful bean varieties.

MOONSTRUCK CHOCOLATIER

∗ ∗ ∗

"One sad fact stood out. In 94 percent of today's chocolate, the cocoa bean of old has been replaced by a bean that has little character.

"The best cocoa beans, when properly prepared, yield chocolate with qualities that verge on the mystical. Disregarding cost, Moonstruck Chocolatier begins with its unique blend of chocolate, then enhances it with the freshest flavors and the creativity that has come to characterize the Pacific Northwest. Award-winning wines, robust espressos, fresh creams, wholesome fruits, and distilled brandies have all brought worldwide acclaim to the region called home by Moonstruck Chocolatier.

"Moonstruck's elegant creations are meant to celebrate the purity of olde-worlde chocolate and the whimsical spirit of life."

The chocolates live up to the sales and marketing pitch and are produced with great care and attention, albeit on a semi-industrial scale. These chocolates may not really be the vehicle for launching fine flavor beans on the American market, but if they help raise questions in the mind of the chocolate lover about the origin of the cocoa beans, they have already won half the battle.

The maître chocolatier is Robert Hammond, who apprenticed under a master chocolatier in the southern United States; after which he studied in France, and completed his European tour by working in Italy, the Netherlands, the United Kingdom, and the Middle East. Returning to the United States, he worked in many top hotels before becoming chef at the Vanderbilt Estate. Hammond is now a leading expert in the field of chocolate.

NEUHAUS
✴ ✴

Postbox 2, B-1602 Vlezenbeek, Belgium
Tel: (32-2) 568 2211 Fax: (32-2) 568 2207
www.neuhaus.be

Neuhaus is surely one of the most famous Belgian chocolate makers. Dating back to 1857, it was started by Jean Neuhaus, a Swiss from Neuchâtel who settled in Belgium, and whose grandson claims to have invented the "praline." Neuhaus opened his first shop, which was, in fact, an apothecary, with his brother-in-law. Marshmallows, licorice, and squares of bitter chocolate were sold as aids to digestion. After his brother-in-law died, Jean Neuhaus developed the chocolate side of the business, with the help of his son Frédéric. The shop rapidly gained a reputation for fine confectionery. Among the famed specialties were fruit pastes, vanilla chocolate, caramels, and "praslines"—a kind of caramelized almond without chocolate. 1895 saw the opening of the first exclusive chocolate shop in Brussels, "Confiserie et Chocolaterie Neuhaus-Perrin."

The company was kept in the family and passed down the generations until 1978, when it was sold and developed into the multinational business, NV Neuhaus Mondose SA.

❦ TASTING NOTES ❦

Only 20 percent of Neuhaus chocolates are handmade; the remaining 80 percent are mass-produced, machine-made confections that smell very sweet and are large in size. White chocolate dominates the selection.

"NEUHAUS" OVAL: this rum truffle had good dark couverture and several layers of avocaat cream that was very sweet, fluid, and buttery.

DARK "N:" this had crunchy nuts and a praline layer.

WHITE CHOCOLATE: this had a "fresh cream" center that was very sweet.

HOUSE SPECIALTIES: Caprice, Tentation, Marron, truffles, and chocolates made with fresh cream and alcohol. There are also 65 varieties of praline.

COUVERTURES USED: Callebaut.

NOKA CHOCOLATE
✦ ✦ ✦

2040 W. Spring Creek Pkwy 138, Plano, Texas 75023, USA
Tel: (214) 764 4077
www.nokachocolate.com

Canadian founders Noah Houghton and Katrina Merrem moved to Texas in 2004, where they launched their Noka chocolate business. Their desire was to reinstate chocolate as "the food of the gods." With their minimalist presentation, tiny origin chocolate squares, and jewelry-like prices, Noka offer a quite unique approach to the world of fine chocolate.

Noka have seen success in the United States where their products were presented as gifts to nominees at the 2004 Golden Globe awards. They were also rated as the number one luxury chocolate by a U.K. daytime TV satellite program—perhaps not the greatest claim to fame?

❧ TASTING NOTES ❧

This was interesting, if rather strong, origin chocolate, with truffles made from each origin variety, and no added lecithin or vanilla. The tiny squares certainly made the chocolate seem as valuable as gold, but there was hardly enough of each to judge the flavor properly.

ORIGIN SQUARES: although there were some good flavors here, the chocolate was not so well balanced and perhaps over-roasted. The Ecuador had the most interest, with a butter note reminiscent of Amedei.

TRUFFLES: unfortunately these seemed to have dried and split quite easily. The flavors and quality of the ganache were good, but the astonishingly high price made the damage just that bit more noticeable.

HOUSE SPECIALTIES: the Signature Box, crafted from polished stainless steel.

COUVERTURES USED: couverture manufactured to Noka's very strict specifications.

OBERWEIS
★ ★ ★

19 Grand-Rue, L-1661, Luxembourg
Tel: (352) 47 07 03 Fax: (352) 49 31 41
www.oberweis.lu

This confissier, pâtissier, and glacier has become one of the great institutions in Luxembourg. Founded in 1964 by Pit Oberweis, joined now by his two sons, the business has expanded to a point that they have had to relocate their production to a purpose-built unit. The latest venture also has a small restaurant, which seats 100 people and serves light meals. Oberweis now has five shops in the Grand Duchy, employing 90 staff members, and has been honored with membership of the prestigious Relais Desserts.

🍷 TASTING NOTES 🍷

HOUSE SPECIALTIES: Speculoos, Printen, Baseler, Leckerli, Spitzkuchen, Stollen, Bambkuch, and marzipan figures.

COUVERTURES USED: Valrhona for the ganache centers, and Lindt for dipping and molded truffle shells.

ORTRUD MÜNCH CARSTENS
★ ★ ★ ★

425 East 58th Street, New York, NY 10022, USA
Tel: (212) 752 9591

Ortrud Carstens has carved a niche in the highly specialized chocolate market in New York since opening her business in 1987. She uses only the finest ingredients and couverture available, and everything is made with meticulous care. Where possible, fresh organic produce is used: unsweetened fruit purées and herb infusions. The tea used in the Earl Grey truffle comes from Marriage Frères in the rue Bourg-Tibourg in Paris's fourth arrondissement: in my opinion the best tea house in the world, and well worth a detour. The finest vanilla is shipped from Tahiti, fresh cinnamon sticks are used, and rare coffee beans are freshly infused. The super-fresh chocolates are distributed daily through carefully chosen gourmet food retailers and selected caterers. Carstens' philosophy is to "create bonbons which are high in cocoa, and low in sugar, thus enabling you to experience the full flavor of the chocolate, with all its subtle floral, fruity, herbal, or spicy nuances and overtones. No matter what type of chocolate

❦ TASTING NOTES ❦

From round wafers of bitter chocolate topped with strips of tangy orange peel, dried cranberry, or stem ginger to hand-cut slices of dried Bartlett pears from the orchards of western California—these were beautifully presented and delicately flavored.

CHOCOLATE-DIPPED PEARS: these paper-thin slices of pear had been half dipped in an explosively fruity dark couverture, which harmonized perfectly with the natural acidity and grainy texture of the fruit. An outstanding and original combination.

EARL GREY TRUFFLES: these were masterful in their fragrance and delicacy—perfect harmony between chocolate, cream, and scented tea.

HOUSE SPECIALTIES: truffles, palet, custom-molded and handcrafted artistic chocolate pieces, dipped fruit, and special molds for Thanksgiving, Christmas, and Valentine's Day.

COUVERTURES USED: exclusively Valrhona, especially the Grand Cru ones made from rare bean varieties.

bonbon, the inherent multidimensional character of the couverture is never overpowered by any added flavors: it is the graceful marriage of chocolate and the other natural ingredients of the highest order."

To balance her seriously purist attitude to chocolate, Ortrud Carstens also makes the most delightful whimsical creations—including "rusty" chocolate tools—needless to say out of the world's finest couverture. For her work she has picked up numerous citations, including Best Chef in America in 1990. She presents in-depth seminars on chocolate making for private clients, as well as to the popular and trade press. Other projects include: commissions such as white chocolate calla lilies with stem ginger stamens; a hand-rolled chocolate cigar filled with champagne ganache, made for a famous American couturier; and a number of other pieces commissioned by designers from Europe and the United States.

PALAIS DU CHOCOLAT
☆ ☆ ☆

1200 19th Street NW, Washington DC 20036, USA
Tel: (202) 659 4244 Fax: (202) 723 8970

With his high-quality French chocolates and pâtisseries, the maître chocolatier at Palais de Chocolat, Dominique Leborgne, quickly established a niche market. He has a wholesale production unit in Tacoma Park, Maryland, which supplies, among others, the Ritz-Carlton and Jean-Louis at the Watergate.

Leborgne had a thorough and star-studded training in France, winning gold medals at the Grand Prix Internationale de la Chocolaterie in France, the World Gastronomic Exhibition in Frankfurt, and numerous others. He has also trained at Dalloyau Gavillon and was head pastry chef at the Intercontinental in Paris; after which he was invited to Washington to open the Willard Intercontinental. He has introduced European chocolate technology and has one of only two German chocolate-coating conveyor belts in the United States.

Importing only the finest chocolates from France and Belgium, Leborgne maintains his roots in the French tradition, visiting France several times a year to keep in touch with professional colleagues and new developments.

❧ TASTING NOTES ❧

These chocolates were shiny and beautifully finished—a real tribute to the care invested in each individual piece.

RASPBERRY: a flat, tombstone-like chocolate finished with cocoa encased a very subtle, smooth, almost liquid raspberry ganache.

AMARETTO: this was a very sweet milk chocolate ganache that had a good texture and delicate amaretto flavor.

COFFEE: this dark chocolate coffee ganache was smooth and buttery.

VALENTIN: a dark chocolate heart was filled with a smooth but rather bland caramel ganache.

SCOTTISH TRUFFLE: this chocolate log, dusted in powdered sugar, contained a milk truffle flavored with Scotch whiskey.

WILD TRUFFLE: a cocoa-dusted light fluffy truffle, this was very smooth and buttery, but lacking in chocolate.

EARL GREY: this was my favorite—an extremely delicately perfumed, creamy and sweet, and well-balanced tea ganache.

HOUSE SPECIALTIES: seasonal specialties include molded figures and fruit paste.

COUVERTURES USED: Callebaut, Cacao Barry, and Valrhona's Guanja and Caraque.

He explains the difference between mass-produced and artisan chocolate as, whatever the time of year, "We make it day by day, but the big factories are already preparing for next Christmas." In the early days of Palais du Chocolat he would even turn down orders, believing that slow, steady growth was preferable to risking a decline in quality for rapid profit. Dominique Leborgne is truly a perfectionist to the end.

PAUL A. YOUNG FINE CHOCOLATES
★ ★ ★ ★

33 Camden Passage, Islington, London N1 8EA, UK
Tel: (44-20) 7424 5750
www.payoung.net

Paul Young has been an enthusiastic and energetic presence around the British chocolate scene for some years. Having been head pastry chef for Marco Pierre White for six years, Paul went on to become a regular on UKTV's *Good Food Live.* He has developed chocolates for Rococo, Pierre Marcolini, and Charbonnel et Walker, as well as consulting for the food industry on new quality products.

Paul seems to have worked with just about everybody in British chocolate—professional or amateur—and, with the help of his business partner, James Cronin, he finally fulfilled his ambition to open his own fine chocolate shop in April 2006. Nestling in the historic Camden Passage near Islington's Upper Street, famous for its antiques shops and market, the boutique-style shop is full of character and a welcome relief in the chocolate desert of North London.

Using fine couverture, entirely natural ingredients, and unusual flavors, Paul A. Young Fine Chocolates is the most recent of the new British fine chocolate shops, and an excellent addition to London's growing reputation as a center of chocolate excellence.

❦ TASTING NOTES ❦

A well-crafted, rich selection of truffles made with quality couverture.

SEA SALTED CARAMEL: this was the highlight—soft and light without being too liquid, with just the right amount of salt. It won a gold award at the Academy of Chocolate Awards 2005.

TRUFFLES: the passion fruit heart was piquant and sharp; the cocoa-dusted plain truffle made from Amedei couverture was just right; and a butter praline with a white chocolate base was a delight to eat.

CARDAMOM GANACHE: made with Amedei Chuao chocolate, this was excellent—not too strong and a fantastic flavor combination.

HOUSE SPECIALTIES: Rose Petal Masala Pave, and a gentleman's chocolate collection that uses masculine flavors such as sandalwood and cedarwood. Pâtisserie specialties include Manjari and Lavender Mille Feuille, and the award-winning sea salted milk chocolate caramel Friande.

COUVERTURES USED: Valrhona and Amedei.

PELTIER
✯✯✯✯

66 Rue de Sèvres, 75007 Paris, France
Tel: (33-1) 47 34 08 62

6 Rue Saint-Domenique, 75007 Paris, France
Tel: (33-1) 47 05 50 02

Peltier was founded in 1880 and quickly became famous for its sorbets. Peltier is a relative newcomer to the world of chocolate, not starting its artisan chocolate production until 1978. Since 2002, it has been home to the Michelin-starred chef pâtissier, Philippe Conticini, who enjoys experimenting as "head of creation and taste." Peltier offers delicious lunches and desserts as well as its range of chocolates.

> ### ❦ TASTING NOTES ❦
>
> HOUSE SPECIALTIES: Muscadine truffles, Sèvrelinettes, and Lucien. Special commissions are also accepted. Seasonal specialties include Father's Day pipes and tools, and masks and clowns for carnivals.
>
> COUVERTURES USED: Valrhona and Cacao Barry.

PIERRE HERMÉ
★ ★ ★ ★ ★

72, Rue Bonaparte, 75006 Paris, France
Tel: (33-1) 43 54 47 77
www.pierreherme.com

185, Rue de Vaugirard, 75015 Paris, France
Tel: (33-1) 47 83 89 96
www.pierreherme.com

Pierre Hermé is known as the "Picasso of Pastry." He began his career at the age of 14, as an apprentice to master pâtissier, Gaston Lenôtre; followed by 11 years as a chef pâtissier for Fauchon, and two years at Ladurée. His first shop opened in Tokyo in 1998 to international acclaim, and there are now five shops in total.

Pierre is constantly experimenting with new textures, flavors, and taste combinations. There is a chocolate for every mood and occasion, and his creations are original without being eccentric.

🍫 TASTING NOTES 🍫

HOUSE SPECIALTIES: a huge, top-quality range: traditional chocolate bonbons, candied fruits, nuts, and coffee; "Absolument Chocolat"— miniature chocolates in the shape of fingers; single-origin and flavored bars; and classical and creative filled chocolates—Mathilda, Aztec, and Choc Chocolat are exquisite.

COUVERTURES USED: Valrhona.

PRALUS
★ ★ ★ ★

8, Rue Charles de Gaulle, 42300 Roanne, France
Tel: (33-477) 712 410 Fax: (33-477) 715 207
www.chocolats-pralus.com

François Pralus grew up in an apartment above his family's shop in Roanne, a small town on the Loire River in the Rhône-Alpes region of France. There, his father, Auguste Pralus, opened his pâtisserie shop in 1948. In 1955 he invented his "praluline"—a praline brioche made with toasted and pink sugar-coated almonds and hazelnuts—which has since been widely copied. Auguste won numerous national accolades for his work, then in 1986 he handed the business over to his son, François.

Before taking over the family business, François studied and worked with pastry chefs and chocolatiers as he traveled around the world. From Brazil to Paris, he worked in renowned restaurants, undertaking an internship at the chocolate department of the Ecole Lenôtre in Paris. Most significant though was his first master, Bernachon, in Lyon. Inspired by this great artisanal chocolate maker, when François returned to Roanne he began to contemplate making his own chocolate, from the bean.

PRALUS

★ ★ ★ ★

François embarked on more world travel: this time to source beans for Pralus' new chocolate-making venture. His travels took him to the Ivory Coast, where a cacao tree was named after him; to Sao Tomé, where he encountered Claudio Corallo's attempts to produce a rare fine chocolate from local African beans; and on to Madagascar, Brazil, and Indonesia.

Pride of place is Pralus' own plantation in Madagascar—39 acres on the Island of Nossy Be, with 44 staff members. The plantation is now producing beans for three different types of Pralus Madagascar chocolate. Pralus also use Madagascan wood for their bonbon boxes. They hope to help the local economy by paying above the average local wage.

Pralus began making chocolate from the bean in 1991, and now have a growing reputation as an origin chocolate maker. They make 18 different origin chocolates from beans from around the world, as well as blends. Pralus also have a range of bonbons and pralines, made with their own chocolate.

❦ TASTING NOTES ❦

The distinctive "leather" flavor notes of Pralus's own chocolate came through in this gift selection—presented in a natural tropical wood box. Some of the ganache chocolates tended to have a "crunchy" texture with noticeable sugar crystals, but this may have come about during transit.

CHOCOLATE-COATED DRIED FRUITS: the orange and apricot were simple but very good, with a pure length.

NUT PRALINES: these worked very well—especially the sugared ganache praline in milk chocolate, shaped like a truffle. The hazelnut crunch slice was also very good.

HOUSE SPECIALTIES: "Pyramide des Tropiques"—a collection of 10g or 50g bars from different single origin beans; and the "Plantation Bar Claudio Corallo"—a chunky, rustic bar with chopped roasted cocoa nibs.

COUVERTURES USED: their own.

PRESTAT
✲ ✲

14 Princes Arcade, Piccadilly, London SW1Y 6DS, UK
Tel: (44-20) 7629 4838
www.prestat.co.uk

One of London's oldest established chocolate houses—first established in 1902 in Oxford Street—Prestat suffered many takeovers and changes of location before re-emerging in Princes Arcade in the 1980s. A decade later, Prestat was sold to Bill Keeling, who has given a long overdue injection of energy to the business. The packaging has been revamped by Kitty Arden.

❦ TASTING NOTES ❦

HOUSE SPECIALTIES: the Connoisseur selection of chocolates, and Brandy Cherries. Their truffle recipe is a family secret that dates back to the time of Napoleon III.

COUVERTURES USED: Belgian.

PUYRICARD
✕ ✕ ✕

Quartier Beaufort, 13090 Puyricard, France
Tel: (33-4) 42 96 11 21 Fax: (33-4) 42 21 47 10
www.puyricard.fr

Belgians by birth, Marie-Anne and Jean-Guy Roelandts came from the Belgian Congo to the Provençal village of Puyricard in 1968. Without any chocolate tradition in their family other than a vacation course in Brussels, they set about learning a new trade and converting the locals, for whom chocolate at that time was restricted to the fringe of their gastronomic traditions, and eaten sparingly only at Christmas. Marie-Anne was in charge of the chocolate, while Jean-Guy took on the difficult task of changing local Provençal tastes. Some 27 years later, Puyricard has grown from a two-person production team to one boasting 26 maître chocolatiers, 70 full-time staff (up to 200 around Christmas), and 11 shops in France that are supervised by Madame Roelandts. The business looks set to remain a family affair as the Roelandts' son and daughter have now joined the team.

Despite her initial grounding in the Belgian tradition, Marie-Anne Roelandts has turned against what she perceives as the overuse of sugar, fats, and the poor quality of raw materials used in her home country. Although the recipes she uses are similar to Belgian ones, the low sugar content is the major distinguishing factor. It is this break with tradition that she feels has led to her success. Using no long-life cream, dehydrated butter, preservatives, or freezing, she says, "I want to arrive at a quality of 100 percent. Others may be happy with 70 percent and everything's OK. But that doesn't interest me at all."

PUYRICARD
✳ ✳ ✳

🍫 TASTING NOTES 🍫

In the well-presented box, the chocolates looked superb: gleaming and in tiptop condition. A high proportion were molded shells—favored because it means very light and fluid centers can be used to fill the chocolates. The chocolate itself was very smooth.

BELGIAN-STYLE CHOCOLATES: in spite of the praiseworthy lack of sugar, these chocolates owe a lot to the Belgian tradition in terms of their couvertures and fillings. I tasted the very smooth and buttery palet d'or, a milk chocolate heart, and the caramel, marzipan, and pralines, which were all very rich and well made.

HOUSE SPECIALTIES: a wide range of chocolates—92 different varieties in all. Most of the chocolates are hand molded rather than enrobed, and any foil wrapping is also done by hand. Two Provençal specialties are the Clou de Cézanne (Cézanne's nail)—a crystallized fig and marc de Provence in a C-shaped chocolate; and Lou Poutounet (a little kiss)—a light filbert praline in milk or dark chocolate. A seasonal specialty (mainly for the summer as it gets very hot and chocolate sales slow down) is the Calisson—a typical sweetmeat from this area of Provence. It is made from the local almonds and candied fruits, or melon and orange peel, and lemon juice in flat oval shapes, with royal icing on top and rice paper underneath.

COUVERTURES USED: made especially by Callebaut. The milk is made from Javan or Madagascan beans; the dark from South and Central American criollo and trinitario beans, blended with a little African forastero.

RICHARD DONNELLY FINE CHOCOLATES
✳ ✳ ✳ ✳

1509 Mission Street, Santa Cruz, California 95060, USA
Tel / Fax: (408) 458 4214
www.donnellychocolates.com

The business was founded in 1988, with the idea of selling by mail order only. This proved to be very seasonal, and soon the retail and wholesale side of the business was expanded. After following in his father's footsteps and studying law for a year at Ripon College, Wisconsin, Richard Donnelly soon realized that this was not the path he wished to tread. He moved to Europe to begin his chocolate-making career at La Varenne's school in Paris. After less than five months, he became an apprentice there, and concluded his studies with the crowning glory of being accepted as an apprentice by Wittamer in Brussels.

On returning to the United States, Donnelly spent a season as chocolate maker and assistant pastry chef with Jean-Yves Duperret at the Nouvelle Pâtisserie in San Francisco. Although he had a thorough grounding in chocolate making in Europe, it was Duperret who really caught Donnelly's imagination,

making cakes that surpassed even the finest in Europe. Hence, fired with enthusiasm, Donnelly had the idea of setting up a chocolate company. It operated from his mother's kitchen in Boston, eventually moving west to Santa Cruz, and Richard Donnelly is now one of the bright young American chocolatiers to watch out for.

Donnelly is famous for his bite-sized bars of chocolate that have a sophisticated wrapping and an exciting array of flavors. Each bar is wrapped in one of a number of Japanese-inspired handmade papers, in the earthy colors of light green, brown, gray, burgundy, or black. The size of the bar (12 ounces) is perfect—just enough to share with a few discerning friends. The bars look beautifully smooth and shiny. Donnelly coats the inside of the mold with a fine layer of chocolate; after which, the mixture is poured in. Because of the fine outer layer, the integrity of the filling is retained, and there are no telltale bits sticking through the bar.

RICHARD DONNELLY FINE CHOCOLATES
★ ★ ★ ★

❦ TASTING NOTES ❦

Since the first edition of this book, Donnelly has added a selection of molded chocolates to its range, with less hand-dipped work. These complement the previous range very well, as do the truffle-shape chocolate liqueurs, which are not too sweet.

CHOCOLATE-DIPPED AUSTRALIAN APRICOT: turtle-shaped and sticky when unwrapped, the chocolate smelled very good and contained a very large, rather sweet, and juicy apricot.

TAHITIAN VANILLA: a molded leaf shape chocolate with a distinct vanilla taste, this was subtly different from the Bourbon vanilla more commonly used, with a note of almond.

WHITE CHOCOLATE MACADAMIA NUT: this was a very fine white chocolate which, unusually, was not excessively sweet.

CHIPOTLE: chili has become a very fashionable flavor for chocolate, but here Donnelly has created an interesting variation using smoked chipotle. The chocolate was certainly strong, but had depth as well as bite.

FILBERT GIANDUJA: this lozenge-shaped milk chocolate had dense but soft ganache with

tiny pieces of freshly ground mild coffee. The slight bitterness balanced well with the milk, and both tastes blended very well as the truffle quickly melted in the mouth. It had a perfect consistency, too!

CHOCOLATE TRUFFLES: these properly handmade truffles with their elongated, uneven shapes wrapped in foil, were covered with fragrant cocoa powder.

DOUBLE-DIPPED MACADAMIA NUT: the Macadamias had been dipped first in white and then in plain chocolate that combined excellently with a slightly salty nut. It had a good, bitter aftertaste, and the nuts had a firm but soft texture, which made it very agreeable to bite into.

HOUSE SPECIALTIES: chocolate lip balm; Donnelly also stocks fine couverture from Callebaut and Valrhona that can be used for eating, baking, or chocolate making. Seasonal specialties include chocolate wine bottles filled with an assortment of either truffles or chocolate almonds.

COUVERTURES USED: Valrhona, Callebaut, and Cacao Barry.

RICHART
★ ★ ★ ★ ★

258 Boulevard St Germain, 75007 Paris, France
Tel: (33-1) 45 55 66 00
www.richart.com

The history of Richart began in Lyon in 1925 when Joseph Richart opened his chocolate boutique in the heart of Old Lyon, on the Croix Rousse hill. A new era began in 1987 when Joseph's son Michel took over the business and added some extra design flair, giving each chocolate a unique design related to its flavor. The chocolates are presented in fashion house packaging, arranged like jewelry in white drawers in a couture box.

❧ TASTING NOTES ❧

The full range of Richart flavors can be sampled in the "Petits Richart Intense" collection of miniature ganaches and pralines—from pure origin ganaches to very fine pralines, flavored with berries, citrus, herbs, flowers, or spices. With 49 tiny examples to choose from, it was hard to pick out highlights, but the collection acts almost as a guide to all the flavorings possible in chocolate.

GANACHES: the mandarin was fresh and intense; while the basil was subtle, but at the same time had a little spice at the front of the tongue. The neroli (orange flower) ganache was a dark delight.

CURRY PRALINE: this was well balanced and not overpowering.

HOUSE SPECIALTIES: the Petits Richart—4 gram (0.14 ounces) chocolates organized in seven aromatic families: balsamic, roasted, fruit, citrus, herbal, floral, and spiced. Each family has seven different fillings.

COUVERTURES USED: their own couverture, made specially for Richart.

ROBERT E's CHOKLAD

★ ★ ★ ★

Odengatan 72, 11236 Stockholm, Sweden
Tel: (46-8) 650 45 23
www.robertes-choklad.com

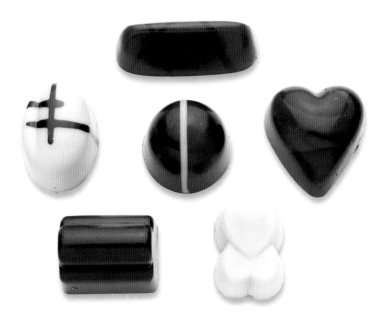

The son of a baker, Robert Eriksson fell in love with the chocolatier's art after his formal training as a pastry chef and baker. At 23, he opened a small chocolate shop and bakery in the center of Stockholm. Sweden has recently undergone a revolution in chocolate, with growing interest in the quality end of the market. This prompted Robert to sell his combined pâtisserie store in 2004 and reopen in 2005 at a new upmarket location. The new shop is devoted entirely to chocolate, and there Eriksson works with the help of chocolatier Josefin Zernell. The shop features space for tastings and a chocolate lounge—an oasis for Stockholm's growing fine chocolate community.

🍫 TASTING NOTES 🍫

A fine collection of superior if chunky ganaches and pralines in a modern style.

GANACHES: the cardamom was a light caramel ganache with a subtle flavor, and the elongated dark pyramid contained a chili ganache with a dark bite. Violet salty liquorice was a very daring combination, but the light caramel ganache in a heart-shaped mold with swirled dark and milk chocolate made it all work!

WHITE CHOCOLATE-COATED PRALINE: this had an unusual twist of salt and a long lingering sweet liquorice.

ROCOCO
★★★★

321 Kings Road, London SW3 5EP, UK
Tel: (44-20) 7352 5857
www.rococochocolates.com

I love Rococo. Some chocolate shops are staffed by snooty types more used to serving the aristocracy than devoted food lovers like you and me. Other chocolatiers look good, but serve musty old products at overambitious prices. What Chantal Coady and her partner James have done since 1983 is to make Rococo the name for truly fine chocolates that also happen to be beautifully packaged and sold by the most simpatico staff in London.

To enter either Rococo shop is to lose oneself among the somber heady scents of single estate cacaos. The shops are light, inviting, and sexy; their chocolates gleaming dark and tantalizing behind broad glass counters. Here you will find Chantal's legendary

ROCOCO
★ ★ ★ ★

🍫 TASTING NOTES 🍫

These traditional English hand-dipped chocolates were filled with geranium, raspberry or coffee cream, or pistachio marzipan. The selection also included dipped apricots.

Truffles: the fresh cream truffles ranged from dark chocolate-covered orange to Irish coffee and amaretto. There were also some of the famous handmade "Truffes Maison"—made from Valrhona's Manjari.

House Specialties: Artisan and Grand Cru bars. In summer, Rococo sells physalis (Cape gooseberries) dipped in Caraïbe, and strawberries dipped in white chocolate; at Easter there are Grand Cru rabbits and quail, and eggs filled with different chocolates.

Couvertures Used: Valrhona—truffles made from Manjari; also Caraïbe for dipping.

Manjari house truffles. Shall I stay pure with the plain ones today, or succumb to saffron and cardamom in white chocolate? Choices, choices. Leaning next to the truffles are elegant boxes of chocolate wafers: extraordinarily rich, incredibly slim, and impossible to resist.

Everyone is allowed a favorite product, and mine is the Organic Rococo Artisan bar. The Coady approach is deft and sure, mixing the familiar with the unusual. Dressed in trademark blue and white wrappers, these bars are to this chocolate fantasist what Agent Provocateur is to the female form. Flavors range from Persian Lime and Basil to Pink Peppercorn and Sea Salt. Milk chocolate scented with attar of roses transports you directly to the Grand Turk's harem; dark orange confit to a courtesan's drawing room. Chantal's trick is to wrap these in tobacco pouches that not only keep the chocolate in good nick, but also heighten the sensation of complicit pleasure. —Kevin Gould

SARA JAYNE STANES
✳ ✳ ✳ ✳

517 Old York Road, London SW18 1TF, UK
Tel: (44-20) 8874 8500
www.sarajaynestanes.com

Sara Jayne Stanes' love of chocolate and fine food began when she was at a convent school in London, where the school lunches left much to be desired. In happy contrast, suppers cooked by her mother were inspired occasions and always of exceptional quality. After working for 15 years as a film and television commercial producer, Sara Jayne underwent a "road to Damascus experience" in 1982, which led her to change career and seize the opportunity to indulge her latent passion for food and cooking. As public relations and marketing director of the U.K.-based Academie Culinaire de France, she was surrounded by the likes of Albert and Michel Roux, the three-star Michelin chefs; John Huber, senior lecturer at Thames Valley University; and Ian Ironside, head pastry chef at Gleneagles Hotel. Here Sara not only found inspiration, but was also able to learn firsthand from the experts, who gave their advice unstintingly.

Having perfected the art of making chocolates, Sara Jayne set up production in her kitchen at home. She now uses only Amedei chocolate, organic whipping cream, alcohol (no concentrates), and herbs, spices, and nuts where demanded. Her recipes do not include butter or any other fat or added sugar. Sara hand-dips all her truffles, a task which she says has taken its toll after 20 years; she now suffers from a unique self-inflicted injury: "truffle elbow."

Sara still works by day at the now anglicized Academy of Culinary Arts, and makes her truffles to special order. She is committed to raising awareness of fine chocolate through the Academy of Chocolate—recently launched in the United Kingdom to encourage chocolate lovers to look beyond the label to the provenance of the cocoa beans used to make chocolate.

She has written numerous newspaper and magazine articles as well as two books, including

SARA JAYNE STANES
★ ★ ★ ★

🍫 TASTING NOTES 🍫

This was an original and attractive selection.

TRUFFLES: these were deliciously light and airy with a mousse-like texture, and subtle flavors that complement the Amedei chocolate rather than dominate it. The gold topped chili truffles had a subtle bite at the back of the mouth without being too strong, so you could still taste the chocolate.

"VENUS NIPPLE:" resembling a reverse-color Mont Blanc—white chocolate topped with dark—this was filled with a coffee ganache made from Arabica coffee and coffee liqueur.

MILK GANACHE WITH MALDON SEA SALT: this was delightfully moreish.

HOUSE SPECIALTIES: made to order.

COUVERTURES USED: Amedei.

Chocolate the Definitive Guide (Grub Street, October 1999, foreword by Michel Roux OBE), which won the U.K. Guild of Food Writers' Jeremy Round Award 2000, and was named "Best Book in the English Language" in the 2000 World Cookbook Fair Awards in Perigueux.

Sara Jayne lives in a Victorian house in Clapham, south west London, with her wine merchant husband, Richard, and Cocoa, their Battersea dog.

SCHAETJENS
★ ★ ★

21 Rue des Trois Cailloux, 80000 Amiens, France
Tel: (33-3) 22 91 32 73 Fax: (33-3) 22 92 26 18

The Lenne family has run its chocolate house for three generations now, and the site of the business has been occupied by professional confectioners since 1767. There are currently 14 employees in addition to Monsieur Lenne, the maître chocolatier—who has been a chocolatier since 1957—and his wife, who joined him in 1965 to help with the running of the business.

❦ TASTING NOTES ❦

RECTANGULAR DARK CHOCOLATE WITH THREE DARK LINES: this was an extremely good sweet praline.

ROUND DARK CHOCOLATES: one had a piece of peel on top and was filled with a very sweet orange almond marzipan; while the other had two stripes on top and an excellent dark whipped ganache within.

CHERRY IN BRANDY: this had no stalk but a stone, so beware—extremely potent alcohol.

WALNUT-TOPPED MILK CHOCOLATE: this was filled with a walnut marzipan—personally, I would have preferred this with dark chocolate to balance the walnut.

HOUSE SPECIALTIES: the Millennium Angel which has been created in homage to Amiens cathedral; the Saleika—a creation of Monsieur Lenne, this is a cherry soaked in fine champagne brandy for one year prior to being dipped in chocolate; and pralines—both filbert and almond. There is a wide range of Christmas specialties on offer; and at Easter, handmade praline eggs are, unusually, made to order on the premises—the taste is incomparable to those made in a factory.

COUVERTURES USED: Valrhona's extra bitter, Café Noir, and the milk Superalpina; Cacao Barry's extra bitter Guyaquil; and Mi-amère.

SLITTI
★ ★ ★ ★

Via Francesca Sud 1268, 51015 Monsummano Terme (PT), Italy
Tel / Fax: (39-572) 640 240
www.slitti.it

Andrea Slitti's father opened the coffee-roasting house Caffè Slitti in 1969, but the young Andrea—while delivering coffee to customers, mainly confectioners and coffee shops—instead became fascinated by chocolate. In 1986, the roasting house was relocated to much larger premises, and a coffee shop was added. Finding himself with extra space, Andrea Slitti took the opportunity to create his own chocolate workshop.

Although Slitti received some formal training in chocolate making, he refers to himself as a self-taught man, having acquired practically all of his knowledge by spending whole days and nights in his workshop. Very quickly, he mastered the art, and he started to create "wild and wonderful" objects in chocolate. Word quickly spread: articles appeared in the press, and gourmet food lovers soon began to arrive. Slitti has been much in demand as a teacher, but steadfastly refuses to leave his shop and his chocolate creations. However, he generously devotes 10 days a year to pupils in his own workshop, where he demonstrates the basics of working with chocolate, and also teaches the history of cocoa and the different cocoa varieties available.

In October 1993, after much coercion by his contemporaries, Slitti was persuaded to take part in the International Show held in Laragne, France. He walked away with the gold medal, beating all 43 participants. This victory—the first time an Italian had won such a prize in France—gave him the right to take part in the final of the Grand Prix International de la Chocolaterie, the biennial event held in Paris. Again, Slitti won the Grand Prix for his artistic presentation, in competition with French, English, Spanish, American, and Japanese chocolatiers.

With masterpieces such as charming, whimsical antique tools made from chocolate and "rusted" with cocoa powder, Slitti pushes the medium of chocolate to its limit, and he certainly stole the show at the Perugia Chocolate Festival in 1994. His chocolates are visually stunning—the work of a fine craftsman.

🍫 TASTING NOTES 🍫

The flavors in this selection were interesting and on the whole very subtle, if rather sweet—especially the milk chocolate snowman, a hazelnut-topped gianduja.

Nut Cluster: with toasted rice crispies, this was excellent.

Oblong Praline: this beautiful burlap-imprinted chocolate also had a bit of rice crispy.

Truffle: this was well dipped, with a sweet, rum flavored center.

Tea Truffle: finely sprinkled with bits of dried tea, this was very good but a bit sweet.

Coffee: reminiscent of tiramisu (the Italian dessert), this had a very strong, fresh, sweet coffee taste.

Squares: the milk square with its speckled-hen finish contained mandarin and Napoleon brandy; the Truffe d'or too much Chartreuse; and the milk square with almonds had an amaretto flavor which was also almost overpowering.

High Percentage Bars: these were interesting and quite tolerable despite their strength; particularly the 90 percent cocoa solids Tropicale bar—made with Arriba beans from Ecuador—which had an excellent length.

House Specialties: "rusty tools," chocolate-covered espresso beans, and chocolate sculptures to order—including a chicken and a teapot.

Couvertures Used: their own, made from cocoa liquor.

SPRÜNGLI
✷ ✷ ✷

Bahnhofstrasse 21, Postfach 8022, 8001 Zurich, Switzerland
Tel: (41-44) 224 46 46 Fax: (41-44) 224 47 35
www.spruengli.ch

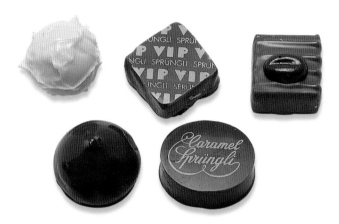

Sprüngli, not to be confused with Lindt & Sprüngli, must be one of the oldest and most famous chocolate establishments in the world. It was started in 1836 by David Sprüngli and is still run by the family today, now into the sixth generation of Sprünglis. The 60-year-old David Sprüngli acquired Vogel's confectioners in Martgasse from the widow Vogel—whose shop had been in existence since 1720—and, with his 20-year-old son Rudolf, founded Confiserie Sprüngli. In 1859, the shop relocated to Paradeplatz, now in the center of the famous shopping area. By 1870 the chocolate side of the business had outgrown the small atelier in the shop premises on Paradeplatz, so production moved to Werdmuhle.

In 1892, Rudolf Sprüngli divided the two sides of the business between his two sons: Johann Rudolf Sprüngli, who took over the chocolate factory, now known as Lindt and Sprüngli; and David Robert Sprüngli who continued the confectionery business in the Paradeplatz. The original building was reconstructed in 1909, and the very first tea room in Zurich opened. In those days, it was uncommon for ladies to go anywhere without a male escort, and Sprüngli can be held partly responsible for the relaxing of this tradition— giving the ladies of Zurich an opportunity to take tea or chocolate with their friends away from the rarefied atmosphere of their homes. Today the café is as popular as ever, being *the* place to meet. It still offers a unique opportunity to simultaneously indulge in the array of cakes and exchange hot gossip.

SPRÜNGLI
★ ★ ★

The original samples tasted were from the Top Ten selection—including truffles and the famous triangular kirsch chocolate, oozing liquid caramels, and nutty pralines.

SWISS SELECTION: the chocolates from this archetypal collection were all incredibly fresh, delicate, not too strongly flavored, and very accomplished.

RECENT ADDITIONS: the Sprüngli range now includes the Grand Cru origin truffle selection—where the Maracaibo particularly shone; and "Cru Sauvage"—plain truffles made with a wild cacao from Bolivia.

HOUSE SPECIALTIES: Truffes du Jour, Champagne Truffle, Coconut and White Chocolate Truffle; and a range of liqueur centers. Seasonal specialties are made for Christmas, Easter, and Valentine's Day.

COUVERTURE USED: Lindt & Sprüngli.

Sprüngli clings to its tradition of artisan-produced chocolates and cakes, and although the production is now geared to vast quantities, the attention to detail and the quality of the raw ingredients remains the core philosophy; only the best and freshest ingredients are used. Their celebrated Truffes du Jour are produced daily from chocolate, cream, and butter: they are guaranteed never to be more than 24 hours old. Thanks to over 150 years of expertise in the field of chocolate making, Sprüngli has a finely tuned stock-control system, which is almost instinctive—rarely do they run out, and overproduction is unusual.

Sprüngli is also most thoughtful concerning any Zurich ex-patriots and other aficionados of their delicious confections. Parcels of chocolate mailed to destinations all over the world are guaranteed to arrive within 24 hours of their despatch. A flourishing relationship between Sprüngli and Federal Express has helped to boost exports in this specialist and rapidly expanding area of the business.

WILLIAM CURLEY
★★★★

10 Paved Court, Richmond, Surrey TW9 1LZ, UK
Tel: (44-20) 8332 3002
www.williamcurley.co.uk

William Curley is a quiet perfectionist. At 33, he has won seemingly endless accolades as pastry chef, including a gold award at the Culinary Olympics in Germany, 2004. With a background in Michelin-starred establishments, William has worked with many renowned chefs: Marco Pierre White at The Restaurant, Pierre Koffmann at La Tante Claire, and Raymond Blanc at Le Manoir aux Quatre Saisons. He also spent three years at the Savoy, London, as chef pâtissier.

It is lucky for chocolate that William spent 10 years planning before setting up his own pâtissier chocolatier shop. With the help of his Japanese wife Suzue, a respected pâtissier herself, his dreams finally came to fruition in 2006, when they opened a small shop in one of Richmond's charming historic alleys.

William aims to make the very best chocolates he can, and does not compromise on any of his ingredients. He uses the best cream, pure butter, and pure chocolate. The chocolates are all hand dipped, with an unusual forked texture on the bottom and identifying cocoa butter, colored prints on the top.

WILLIAM CURLEY

★ ★ ★ ★

🍫 TASTING NOTES 🍫

This selection contained award-winning ganaches and delicately flavored truffles—including a pure chocolate truffle made from Valrhona's Araguani, and a classic-style, hand-coated truffle flavored with port.

CHUAO: gold winner at the 2005 Academy of Chocolate Awards, this plain ganache made from Amedei's Chuao chocolate had superb butter plum notes. Clean and light with an excellent length, it was marked with a fleck of edible gold leaf. Wonderful!

YUZU: William's Japanese influence comes through here with this ganache flavored with yuzu, a Japanese bitter citrus. The flavor was very refreshing, like grapefruit, with an orangy mandarin depth.

FRESH MINT: this light ganache contained beautifully fresh real mint—not at all bitter.

HOUSE SPECIALTIES: Olympic Gold Medal dessert—chocolate Mille Feuille.

COUVERTURES USED: Valrhona and Amedei.

WITTAMER
★ ★ ★ ★

6-12-13 Place du Grand Sablon, Grote Zavel 12, 1000 Brussels, Belgium
Tel: (32-2) 512 37 42 Fax: (32-2) 512 52 09
www.wittamer.com

Wittamer is another family dynasty akin to the Bernachons in Lyon—except that the chocolate-making side of the business was introduced only relatively recently by the grandson of the original master baker, Henri Wittamer, who founded the enterprise in 1910. Born in Arlon, Belgium, of Austrian parents, he chose to set up his bakery in the Place du Grand Sablon in Brussels. He must have been a man of great vision because this quartier has become one of the chic shopping areas in Brussels, and is now the center of the antiques trade.

The business has expanded considerably over the years, and Wittamer now owns several shops side by side, each with a different specialty: the bakery and pâtisserie, the chocolaterie, the icecreamery, the salon de thé, and the traiteur and gourmet shop. Henri Wittamer's son, Henri-Gustave, is still involved in the management of the company, particularly with the bakery side; while his son Henri Paul (known as Paul), the maître chocolatier, has expanded the ice cream and the pâtisserie areas, and was responsible for inaugurating the chocolate shop in 1988. In 1986, Henri Paul achieved the distinction of being made a member of the prestigious Relais Desserts, winning prizes for his Samba—a masterpiece made up of two contrasting chocolate mousses; and in Japan in 1989, his Akin. Inspired by the Japanese word for autumn, the award-winning Akin is a delicious combination of chestnuts and chocolate.

Paul's sister Myriam started the traiteur (outside catering) and gourmet service in 1985. This has proved a huge success—especially among the international set based at the United Nations and European Union headquarters.

WITTAMER

★ ★ ★ ★

🍫 TASTING NOTES 🍫

These chocolates were rich, buttery, and extremely good.

PALET: with its name printed in cocoa butter, this was a very fine ganache—rich in vanilla, butter, and cream with a good fragrant bouquet.

DARK CHOCOLATE PYRAMID: with a very full fragrant aroma, this had lots of butter, and was not too sweet.

WHITE TRUFFLE: this was very white indeed. It had a dark center, but the white chocolate dominated.

THÉ: the chocolate with the red cocoa butter transfer had a very rich dark chocolate flavor that came through after a fragrant Earl Grey tea.

MOLDED PARCEL WITH A BOW: this caramel ganache was very smooth and buttery.

HOUSE SPECIALTIES: a selection of over 60 varieties of praline, which include ganaches, giandujas, marzipans, truffles, fresh cream chocolates, orange and lemon peel dipped in chocolate, and nougatine. They do seasonal specialties for Valentine's Day, Secretary's Day, Mother's and Father's days, St. Nicholas, Christmas, and New Year; in fact, any excuse to create new and exciting objects in chocolate. As Wittamer is a very small artisan business, it can readily respond to these very specialized feasts.

COUVERTURES USED: made specially for Wittamer by Callebaut in Belgium.

WOODHOUSE CHOCOLATE
✳ ✳ ✳ ✳

1367 Main Street, Saint Helena, CA 94574-1904, USA
Tel: (800) 966 3468 / (707) 963 8413 Fax: (707) 963 8072
www.woodhousechocolate.com

John and Tracey Anderson fell in love with European fine chocolates as teenage students during visits to Belgium and France, while at college in England. Later they returned to work on the Anderson family vineyard in California's Napa Valley, spending the next 20 years creating cabernet, chardonnay, merlot, and a subject of much pride: their sparkling wine.

Tracey Wood had been a budding "foodie" from an early age, and after taking a degree in studio art, she went on to train in pastry at San Francisco's California Culinary Academy. After a short time working in restaurants, she became chef at her husband's family winery, where she also spent 15 years helping to blend the wines. The Andersons' love of fine chocolates did not diminish though, and frequent trips to Europe were required to bring back new supplies.

After 20 years the family decided to sell the winery, and it seemed a natural step to reproduce the quality of chocolates they had tried in Belgium and France. While Tracey spent two years studying in Canada and the United States, and visiting Europe, husband John developed the new business and facilities.

In 2004 Woodhouse Chocolate was launched; the company name deriving from Tracey's maiden name, and the curiously chosen Indian elephant becoming the company emblem. With a look inspired by the film *Chocolat*, the shop was opened in a nineteenth century building in Saint Helena in the Napa Valley. Behind the shop lies the kitchen, where the perfect-looking Woodhouse chocolates are created. John and Tracey use traditional flavors and techniques, as well as the highest quality of fresh ingredients.

WOODHOUSE CHOCOLATE
✷ ✷ ✷ ✷

❦ TASTING NOTES ❦

Influenced by a mixture of Italian and Belgian traditional styles, this was a very fresh, daintily presented collection in a Regency-style blue box. Overall, there was excellent freshness, although the chocolates were perhaps a little sweet when compared to more modern-style chocolatiers.

FIORI SI SICILIA: this featured layers of milk ganache, orange marzipan, and fresh cream—a delightful creation.

QUATRE EPICES: four spices were blended in a ganache, but this was not too sharp.

MINT GANACHE: this was subtle and refreshing.

HONEY BUTTER MOUSSE: this was light, but could have featured a stronger honey.

HOUSE SPECIALTIES: chocolate sea turtles filled with nuts and caramel, and brown butter ganaches.

COUVERTURES USED: E Guittard.

ZELLER CHOCOLATIER
★ ★ ★

Place Longemalle 1, 1204 Geneva, Switzerland
Tel: (41-22) 311 5026

The fairies have long since vanished, but Willy Zeller has discovered their secret and continues to make Pavés Glacés—the little chocolate slabs resembling the old Geneva paving stones—inspired by a fairy tale. His business was established in Geneva in 1959 at 13 Place Longemalle, but it is now housed in a bigger shop on the corner of Place Longemalle and the very fashionable Rue du Rhône. Here, he still models marzipan figurines for the windows, which are decorated by his wife. For the last 20 years, they have been ably assisted by Madame Monique Gimmi and her sister, Madame Brigitte Zentilin. Willy Zeller, the maître chocolatier, did his apprenticeship in Basle between 1936 and 1939, and has worked with many of the finest Swiss chocolatiers. Over the last 32 years, he has also been responsible for training many young chocolatiers.

The legend that was the inspiration for Zeller's famous Pavés Glacés tells of a little girl enjoying the lakeside and watching men hauling quarried paving stones, shaped into cubes by masons, from the sailing boats that had carried them from the other side of the lake. The shiny stones were used in Geneva to build the streets on which horses and carriages rode. One of the two fairies who appeared before the girl was dressed in a pink, vanilla-scented gown. She said, "I am the Sweet Fairy who will make your

✳ ✳ ✳

dreams come true. Every paving stone you take in your hands will turn into chocolate." The second fairy blew gently on the stones and said, "I am the Bise (the name of the wind that blows on the lake, and also the word in French for a kiss) who makes glazed chocolate. Every time you eat chocolate you will think of the sweetness of Geneva and the cool of the lake."

🍫 TASTING NOTES 🍫

A 1950s style box—gold with a champagne-colored suede-effect lid—housed a selection of dark and milk chocolates. There were some very good oranges slices with peel dipped in dark chocolate, and an outstanding pistachio marzipan in dark chocolate. There was plenty of variation in the fillings.

DARK OR MILK CHOCOLATE PAVÉS: without a doubt, these were the best in the selection—very thin, flat, hard pieces of nougatine with almonds, dipped in chocolate. I preferred the milk chocolate to the dark; its creamy taste was the perfect foil to the crunchy brittle inside. These were very good, and especially appealing for those who like hard, nutty centers.

HOUSE SPECIALTIES: pavés glacés; over 70 different types of chocolates; Moules du Lac (mussels from the lake)—large chocolates filled with caramel cream; marzipan figures—people, animals, fruit, vegetables, and flowers; and commissions and seasonal specialties for Christmas, Easter, and Valentine's Day.

COUVERTURES USED: top secret.

OTHER CHOCOLATIERS OF NOTE

Unfortunately it was not possible within the confines of this book to include all the chocolatiers that deserve to be listed—both established houses and the many new chocolatiers that have sprung up since the first edition was published in 1995. Here is just a small sample of the companies worthy of further investigation.

COPPENEUR
Wittichenauer Strasse 15-17,
53604 Bad Honnef, Germany
Tel: (49-22) 249 01 04 0
www.coppeneur.de
Founded in 1993, the company launched its Coppeneur brand in 2002. Recently experimented with chocolate produced for them from beans they have sourced.

DARRICAU
7 Place Gambetta, 33000 Bordeaux, France
Tel: (33-5) 56 44 21 49
www.darricau.com
This third generation shop creates Bordeaux specialties with Valrhona chocolate.

DAUBOS
35, Rue Royale, Quartier Saint Louis,
Versailles, France
Tel: (33-1) 39 50 54 97
www.chocolatsdaubos.com
Stylish award winner and member of the Croqueurs du Chocolat.

DEMEL
Kohlmarkt 14, A-1010 Vienna, Austria
Tel: (43-1) 535 17 17 0
www.demel.at
Traditional Viennese coffee and chocolate house with roots dating back to 1786.

ENRIC ROVIRA
Sant Geroni 17, 08296 Castellbell, El Vilar, Spain
Tel: (34-93) 834 09 27
www.enricrovira.com
Avant-garde chocolatiers, heavily influenced by Barcelona style.

MICHEL BELIN
4, Rue Docteur Camboulives, 81000 Albi, France
Tel: (33-5) 63 54 18 46
www.michel-belin.com
Established for 20 years in Albi, and a store in Toulouse.

ORIOL BALAGUER
Plaza Sant Gregori Taumaturg, 2, 08021
Barcelona, Spain
Tel: (34-93) 201 1846
www.oriolbalaguer.com
Daring flavors and ingredients, such as wasabi and soya.

PATRICK ROGER
108 Boulevard St-Germain, 75006 Paris, France
Tel: (33-1) 43 29 38 42
Modern chocolates and sculpture.

PIERRE CHAUVET ARTISAN CHOCOLATIER
32, Avenue Victor Hugo, 07200 Aubenas, France
Tel: (33-4) 75 35 55 15
Regional flavors and elaborate chocolate squares.

PIERRE MARCOLINI
Avenue Louise 75M, 1050 Brussels, Belguim
Tel: (32-2) 538 42 24
www.marcolini.be
Against the typical sweet Belgian trend, these are fine chocolates with plenty of flare. The company makes a limited amount of its own chocolate.

PLAISIR DU CHOCOLAT
251-253 Canongate, The Royal Mile,
Edinburgh EH8 8BQ, UK
Tel: (44-131) 556 9524
www.plaisirduchocolat.com
Continental style in Scotland. Uses Callebaut couverture.

INDEX